ISSUES THAT CONCERN YOU

Body Piercing and Tattoos

Hester L. Furey, *Book Editor*

GREENHAVEN PRESS

A part of Gale, Cengage Learning

GALE
CENGAGE Learning·

Farmington Hills, Mich • San Francisco • New York • Waterville, Maine
Meriden, Conn • Mason, Ohio • Chicago

GALE
CENGAGE Learning

Patricia Coryell, *Vice President & Publisher, New Products & GVRL*
Douglas Dentino, *Manager, New Products*
Judy Galens, *Acquisitions Editor*

© 2015 Greenhaven Press, a part of Gale, Cengage Learning

WCN: 01-100-101

Articles in Greenhaven Press anthologies are often edited for length to meet page requirements. In addition, original titles of these works are changed to clearly present the main thesis and to explicitly indicate the author's opinion. Every effort is made to ensure that Greenhaven Press accurately reflects the original intent of the authors. Every effort has been made to trace the owners of copyrighted material.

Cover image © iofoto/Shutterstock.com.

LIBRARY OF CONGRESS CATALOGING-IN-PUBLICATION DATA

Body piercing and tattoos / Hester L. Furey, book editor.
  pages cm.—(Issues that concern you)
  Includes bibliographical references and index.
  ISBN 978-0-7377-7238-8 (hardcover)
  1. Body piercing—Juvenile literature. 2. Tattooing—Juvenile literature. I. Furey, Hester Lee.
  GN419.25.B63 2015
  391.6'5—dc23
                                                            2014027561

Printed in the United States of America
1 2 3 4 5 6 7 19 18 17 16 15

CONTENTS

The United States has experienced a kind of "tattoo renaissance" since the last decades of the twentieth century. Nonetheless, popular culture indicates that those who choose these types of body modifications remain susceptible to unkind judgment. Most likely, few viewers were surprised by Dolly Parton's dryly delivered line in the 1989 film *Steel Magnolias* that "the best thing I can say about her is that all of her tattoos are spelled correctly," but as late as 2013, in the film *Meet the Millers*, a young man with a misspelled tattoo ("No Ragrets") was treated as the butt of numerous jokes. That particular misspelling was also featured in a widely circulated Internet meme of poorly chosen and executed tattoos. The general public may no longer assume that individuals with tattoos have done jail time, given in to a drunken impulse, or embraced an antiestablishment lifestyle, but in the place of those old assumptions, two new prejudices have emerged. First, many assume that those with tattoos may have compromised their health by exposure to unsanitary conditions or unsterilized instruments. Second, there is a tendency to view tattoos and other body modifications such as piercing as the choices of immature people with poor judgment. And, in fact, a growing body of regret narratives has emerged as more and more people have tattoos—enough to be studied by scholars in the field of cultural studies.

In the past, mental health professionals tended to place the practices of body piercing and tattooing on a spectrum of self-harming behaviors that ranged from cutting to suicide. Now such attitudes have diminished. While health professionals across the board worry about the possibility of contamination, infection, and patient negligence in the care and cleaning of body modifications, a significant number of physicians and therapists have argued that tattoos and piercings are not self-injurious. In support of this idea, many people who have piercings and tattoos have written eloquently that these practices empowered them in some way, making them feel more in control of their bodies and their personal identities. Cultural critics have supported this perspective, arguing that piercings and tattoos often express involvement in a community.

A 2012 report by the American Medical Association (AMA) established that Americans spend upwards of $2.3 billion annually on tattoos alone; nearly a quarter of Americans have tattoos, with the majority in the eighteen- to thirty-nine-year-old age range (36 percent of adults ages eighteen to twenty-five and 38 percent of adults ages thirty to thirty-nine have tattoos). Nearly a quarter of women have tattoos, compared to 20 percent of men. Some social theorists believe the growing numbers of women getting tattoos, especially larger, more visible work, reflect a rebellion against the appearance standards imposed by the beauty industry and in some way are a response to the wave of feminism that began in the late 1960s to early 1970s.

However, that same AMA report showed a more than 30 percent growth in tattoo removals, which are usually far more expensive than tattoos themselves (tattoos cost an average of a few hundred dollars, depending on the size and number of labor hours involved, whereas removal may take more than ten sessions costing about $200 each). Perhaps many people in the United States feel freer to have tattoos because they believe they can always have them removed if they change their minds. Removal is not guaranteed, though, and often involves scarring. Some inks are easier to remove than others. The AMA report found that blue ink is the hardest to remove. Many tattoo inks contain heavy metals and are known to be toxic; others become toxic during the bodily dispersal that follows tattoo removal. Also, the tattoo removal industry is far less regulated than the tattoo industry, a fact that concerns many health professionals.

Reports on how tattoo and piercing choices affect employment prospects vary from source to source. In general it seems that visible tattoos or uncommon piercings (other than, say, ear and nose piercings) will adversely affect employment prospects, particularly if the employer is a government or health care entity or a small, locally owned business with an older proprietor. Still, led by companies like Google, many private employers are trying to attract talent with more liberalized dress codes and workplace policies. Even now, in many fields, people who are established in their professions tend to have more freedom to do as they wish about body modifications, compared to those just entering the workforce, who encounter more restrictions and resistance. Appearance discrimination in the workplace based on employee choices—rather than membership in a protected category such as race or gender—is still legal. There is a growing sense that as the tattooed and pierced population ages and becomes more normalized, such sights will become less shocking, although the legal history of employment discrimination cases involving body modifications remains mixed.

Views on body piercings and tattoos have changed throughout history. In many indigenous tribal cultures, participation in these ancient practices played an integral part in establishing one's place in society. In Europe and the United States, however, tattoos and body piercings elicited strongly negative responses and were most often associated with antisocial tendencies or with membership in subcultures far outside mainstream norms, such as those of circus performers, gangs, and prison inmates. Since the last half of the twentieth century, these practices have become more widespread in the Western world and are now regarded as part of a range of body modifications, many of which are acceptable.

The authors cited in this anthology discuss the motivations for body modification, as well as the physical and social outcomes of these procedures. In addition, the volume explores how people use tattoos and piercings to communicate something about themselves. *Issues That Concern You: Body Piercing and Tattoos* offers a resource for everyone interested in this issue.

ONE

Tattoos Have Become Mainstream

Susan Swartz

In the following viewpoint Susan Swartz contends that tattoos are becoming more and more popular in US society. The practice is no longer taboo, the author maintains, and has become more mainstream. In the past, tattoos were identified with those on the fringes of society, but they are now worn by people from all walks of life, says the author. People today view tattoos as wearable art and use them to convey messages about identity. Swartz is a freelance writer and author based in Sonoma County, California.

Kate Wilder, a cosmetologist, got her first tattoo when she was 18. Penny Ferry, a retired retailer, got hers when she was 67.

Neither woman was a sailor out on a bender, as might fit the old tattoo mythology, although Wilder's 12 tattoos now include an anchor as a nod to her Navy grandfather.

Ferry has only one, a dragonfly on her wrist, in memory of her daughter, Morgan, who died of cancer at age 38.

Tattoos Are Becoming More Popular

Once the result of a wild night or whim, tattoos have gone mainstream and are now considered wearable art, a permanent accessory and a way to celebrate a milestone, declare your love, flaunt your individuality or honor a loved one.

One in five American adults now has a tattoo, according to a Harris Interactive survey.

In her book "Bodies of Subversion: A Secret History of Women and Tattoo," Margot Mifflin reports tattoos are now favored more by women, with 23 percent of women sporting "tats" and 19 percent of men. And a growing number of the tattooed are middle-aged.

Madame Chinchilla, who runs the Triangle Tattoo Art and Museum in Fort Bragg [California], has been injecting pigment

A mother hugs her son, showing off a tattoo on her wrist. In contemporary culture, people from all walks of life have tattoos.

"9 to 5 Tattoo," cartoon by Marty Bucella, www.CartoonStock.com. Copyright © Marty Bucella. Reproduction rights obtainable from www.CartoonStock.com.

for 27 years. Her clients range in age from 18 to 70, and she thinks the resurgence of interest comes from the media showing off tattooed celebrities and giving "the general public open permission to jump on the bandwagon."

Some tattoo seekers, she said, want to "join the tattoo club" and copy the style of friends and rock stars. More opt for personal expressions, in the form of designs or meaningful quotes.

Chinchilla's most memorable works celebrate a mastectomy or other major scar, like the client who had Chinchilla decorate her mastectomy scar with a redwood branch.

"The tattoo taboo is waning," said Mike Pritchett, owner of Matchless Tattoo in Sebastopol [California], while coloring in a rose on a young woman's arm with a needle that looked like a dentist drill.

"Getting one used to be an edgy outsider thing. Now it's soccer moms and white-collar people," he said, waving to a regular, whose business suit concealed a Japanese painting of koi fish and a waterfall down his back and buttocks.

Tattoos Are a Commitment

Tattoo shops are regulated by the state [California] through a 2-year-old law, the Safe Body Art Act. It's enforced by the Sonoma County Department of Health Services, which issues permits and makes annual inspections through its body art division. . . .

Tattoo artists must complete an Occupational Safety and Health Administration (OSHA) blood-borne pathogen and cross-contamination course, have a current hepatitis B vaccination and "show us a plan on how they're going to keep their facility clean," said Leslye Choate, whose office also covers piercing, permanent cosmetics and branding, which involves burning images onto skin.

"Any time you pierce the skin, there is risk of infection," Choate said. Also, there can be allergic reactions to materials used "and the rare risk of infection of blood-borne diseases, such as HIV and hepatitis."

To date, she said Sonoma County [California] has no reports of cases of HIV or hepatitis associated with tattoos or piercing.

Still, body art doesn't come easy. Tattoos demand a commitment of time, money and certain discomfort. And if you change your mind, they're pricey and often difficult to alter or remove.

Pritchett, who charges $150 an hour for his custom designs, said, "Getting tattooed is a very personal experience. Everyone has a different pain threshold."

The process creates "a large open wound," he said, and takes a week to 10 days to heal. Some parts of the body, like the feet, rib cage, stomach and elbows, are more sensitive than others.

Wilder said her tattoos felt "like a cat scratch that goes on for hours, and after you get it, your skin is red and swollen and you're bleeding. But I have a beautiful piece of art that is mine."

"It hurts for a couple of days," said James Peyton of Santa Rosa [California], whose 1890s-style pin-up girl took three six-hour sessions to complete. He said he's spent "a couple of thousand dollars" on tattoos that include stencils of his three children's tiny handprints decorating his back.

Nina Hari of Occidental [California] has a hibiscus on her left calf that she got at age 64 to celebrate her retirement from teaching. The only negative reviews come from male contemporaries, she said.

"They're horrified," Hari said. "They associate tattoos with soldiers home on leave going to bars and brothels.

"But I like mine. I think it's kind of cool."

TWO

Tattoos Often Represent a Struggle to Survive

Joseph Miller

In the following viewpoint Joseph Miller contends that tattoos helped him retain his sense of identity. He was deployed to Iraq three times as a member of the US armed forces and suffered from post-traumatic stress disorder. The author chose to get tattoos as a reminder of his value system and as a source of strength. Tattoos can be a form of therapy, he asserts, and can be part of the healing process for those who have experienced trauma. At the time of the viewpoint, Miller was a graduate student in Canadian/American history at the University of Maine.

One way that I have fought for my identity, both consciously and intuitively, has been with tattoos. After the suicide bombing I slowly recognized that I could not feel anything but anger. I noticed that I could not develop a close relationship with anyone ([except] other people in my unit) and I was becoming an individual obsessed with instincts and self-preservation. I tried to go to church, but all of the silent prayer made me have flashbacks (my first serious flashbacks came at services) and all I could do was sit there and be angry. I could sense that I was losing who I was and my value system. I had experienced other veterans who began to think of all Arabs or Muslims as terrible. I feared that I might lose my moral compass because of how angry I consistently found myself.

A Fight for Identity

I had seen and experienced what it was like to watch a man's life end and I was afraid that I could never forgive myself if I ever took an innocent life. As a person raised in a religious evangelical family, I was a faithful person. I could no longer endure church

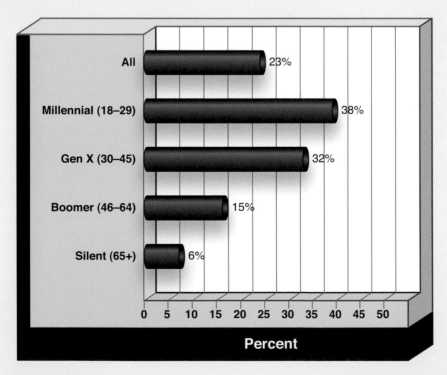

Millennials Are Most Likely to Have Tattoos

Percent of people who have tattoos, by generation

All — 23%
Millennial (18–29) — 38%
Gen X (30–45) — 32%
Boomer (46–64) — 15%
Silent (65+) — 6%

0 5 10 15 20 25 30 35 40 45 50

Percent

Taken from: "Millennials: A Portrait of Generation Next," Pew Research Center, February 2010. http://pewsocialtrends.org.

services, but I wanted to express my values in a way that would constantly remind myself who I was. I started by expressing the hopes that I would never take an innocent life by tattooing a double edge sword and the words god's breath on my firing arm. . . . I had a great desire to never be the agent of the horrible things I saw after the suicide bombing.

There was something really freeing about that experience and it made it easier to grasp who I was. PTSD [post-traumatic stress disorder] as a culturally negotiated and defined soul challenges our ideas about our self, but as a simple neurological phenomenon it damages the place in our brain that manages conscious memory, and identity. Both have extreme impacts on our lives so tattoos can become powerful reminders of who we are when the world that we know falls apart. I recognized the utility of wearing my values on my sleeve, so when I was having trouble conceiving of them I permanently placed [them] on my body.

I recognized that with grace and perseverance any storm could be weathered. There was a simple solution. I tattooed the words on my forearms and recognized that my greatest resource was myself. The left forearm would be perseverance because "the first rule in a knife fight was that you are gonna get cut, get cut in the left forearm" and reinforced my desire for divine help with grace on my firing arm. I deployed again and it was the worst year of my life. I had serious PTSD and mTBI [mild traumatic brain injury], but I was officer and lives depended on my performance.

The Struggle to Come Home

I was broken and worn down, but I had my values on my sleeves. My attitude was terrible but my performance never waned. I could perform my job, but everything was painful. I left the Army bitter and alone. I began blaming myself and thinking that is my fault that I had succumbed to an invisible wound. I began to believe that I was letting soldiers down in Afghanistan. I should be better by now, right? No one would ever concede that I even had any problems because I was articulate and I was in shape. No visible wounds.

A US Army soldier with "loyalty" tattooed on his arm prays before a mission in Afghanistan in 2010. Some people mark themselves with tattoos of images or words that help them to heal.

I began to really despise myself and believe that it was my fault. I was weak, a coward, or immoral. Three tours in Iraq as infantry platoon leader and Iraqi Army Operations officer was not enough service. I was letting my country and soldiers down. . . .

Just like when my world first collapsed I had to give myself a visualization, on my body, that this was not my fault and in a lot of ways I am better. I was beginning to become open, unashamed and even in ways proud of my struggles after my service in Iraq. I read Hemingway's "The world breaks everyone, and afterwards, many are strong at the broken places." Though I did not yet feel strong, I again decided to fight for that idea. To place it on my body as commitment to myself and my identity. I also wanted to use Hemingway because, in the end, he lost his battle with mental illness and took his life. I wanted to be reminded that even in a victorious idea that we, who have had our identity challenged by the crucible of war, have to fight every day to preserve ourselves in spirit and in body. That this is both a neuro-chemical battle and fight for our own souls.

Tattoos Can Be a Form of Therapy

There is nothing wrong with anyone of us who struggle to come home. Tolkien's famous "not all who wander are lost," is such a fitting metaphor for the long road home. I think it is a never ending battle to preserve our identities and I would challenge others by stating that the fight is worth it. If you have this conflict you are not alone, this is not a new problem, you are not weaker and the world needs people who have been broken by trauma. Tattoos are culturally ubiquitous in our generation but they can be a kind of cognitive therapy. An idea that you choose to embrace, even when you don't initially feel it, that changes patterns of behavior and eventually emotions. We can only spend so much time with our therapists, but our greatest resource is ourselves. So fight for yourself as hard as you fought for your country.

I would urge others to share their tattoos stories.

THREE

Body Piercings and Tattoos Can Be a Form of Self-Care

Rebecca Lawrence

In the following viewpoint a woman named Rebecca maintains that tattoos and body piercings can help those with compulsive disorders. The author suffers from dermatillomania, a compulsive skin-picking disorder. She relates her experience with body modification as a teenager and the role that piercings and tattoos play in her life. The author believes that body modification can be empowering and soothing for those with mental illnesses. Rebecca is a member of the Canadian Body-Focused Repetitive Behaviours Support Network.

Ever since I was 16, old enough to legally sign for my own piercing, I would make a change to my body every time there was a major change in my life. Dealing with a break up in high school, I started stretching my ears. Another dramatic change in friendships, I got my eyebrow pierced and had that piercing for 4 years. My parents tend towards the more conservative side of the spectrum, and though they are incredibly liberal and open-minded, piercings and tattoos on my body have always been a sore spot for our relationship.

How many tattoos do you currently have on your body? (percent who said "one or more")

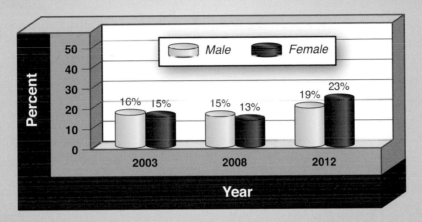

Taken from: Samantha Braverman, "One in Five US Adults Now Has a Tattoo," *The Harris Poll*, no. 22, February 23, 2012. www.harrisinteractive.com.

It's been very difficult to explain the soothing, empowering nature of body modification for someone who finds it very difficult to control the damage they do to their body. My first tattoo, the word "fear" in Greek, Φόβος, has been strategically tattooed on my lower neck. A symbol of the ever-present anxiety that I feel due to various mental illnesses as well as DTM [dermatillomania, a compulsive skin-picking disorder]; it acts as a reminder to be afraid of fear. Will Smith once said, "I'm motivated by fear, fear of fear, I hate being scared to do something". That resonates with me very much. I am afraid of the fear taking over my body again like it has in the past. Afraid of fear built roadblocks in my journey to recovery and self-acceptance.

Piercings and Tattoos Can Allow Healing

After the worst depression I have ever experienced in my life, a depression that ruined relationships and my own academic standards. A depression that caused me to drop out of my University degree in Psychology, a depression that kept me in bed for almost 8 months of my life. I vowed, once the collective efforts of myself and my loved ones pulled me out of this deep void and I returned to school, I would get a tattoo to commemorate the change to the very core of my being. I made the appointment recently for January, and I also proceeded to get my nose pierced.

Piercings and tattoos are a test of will for my hands. The time that they need to heal without any dirty fingers prying, any nails

Body piercings and tattoos can be a form of self-care for some individuals who suffer from certain mental illnesses. For example, sufferers of dermatillomania are forced to stop picking the area while a new piercing or tattoo heals.

searching, with regular cleaning and self-care to promote health. It's as though they allow me to practice the acts of self-care that I neglect on my own if left to my own vices. In the past, I have let wounds become infected on purpose, as a form of twisted self-hatred. Tattoos must not be picked at or else the ink will seep out from under your skin or get disfigured and ruin the design. Because it's such a beautiful piece of art that I really do want to have on my body, it forces my hands down. It helps me keep my hands away from my skin.

I have had many inspiring conversations with my peer support group co-facilitator about DTM, but one particular conversation sticks out in my brain. We were discussing the similarities and differences between Trich [trichotillomania, compulsive hair pulling] and Derma [dermatillomania]. One major difference we noticed, is that I found with dermatillomania, I just have to wait the few weeks for a sore spot to heal over completely, and if I can control myself for that long and don't have any other spots, I can go without picking for a little while. Unlike Trich [TTM], she explained it as being similar to having a horrible addiction take over your body, and your abused substance of choice being right on top of your head at all times.

I know not everyone is into body modifications and of course I respect that. But I hope this invitation into the pits of my brain has helped some people understand why tattoos help me come to terms with the skin around my body. Perhaps, other DTM and TTM sufferers can relate or have been inspired to take their self-care into their "own hands".

Body Modification Can Be a Way to Assert Ownership of One's Body

Olivia James

> In the following viewpoint a woman named Olivia maintains that piercings and tattoos allow people to take ownership over their bodies. Body modification allows people to assert their identity, the author argues, and can help them forge a deeper emotional connection with their body. Tattoos and piercings are especially empowering for traditionally marginalized groups and those people who have powerful negative associations with their bodies, she maintains. Olivia is a social justice blogger in her twenties and owner of the blog *We Got So Far to Go: Social Justice Rants and Raves.*

There are very few ways that we get control over our physical bodies, particularly our appearance. We don't get to choose things like height, build, weight (much), skin tone, eye color and shape, facial features . . . we can barely even control our hair most of the time. And philosophically speaking, people today rarely view their body as really THEM: generally it's considered more of a house for your soul or your mind, broken away from the real

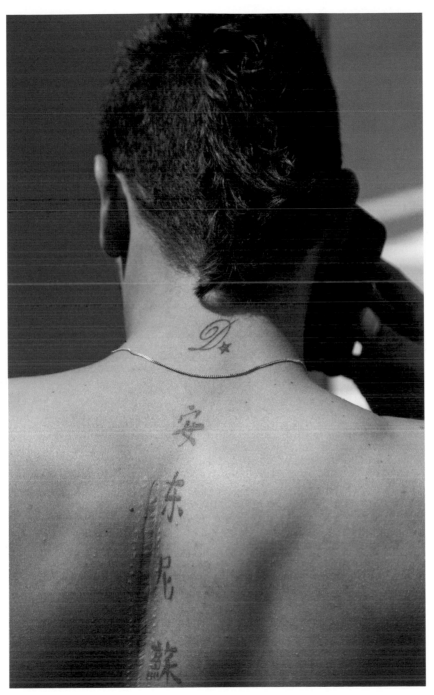

Tattooing on or near the site of body scars can be empowering for some. Tattoos can help reverse the negativity associated with a scar or celebrate an injury that has been overcome.

you. And so it seems to me that asserting ownership over our own bodies is . . . extremely important.

Body Modification Is Empowering

Particularly for traditionally marginalized groups whose bodies are considered public space, having a way to mark your body as your own, or physically change your body in order to feel more in tune with it or to connect it to your emotions is a powerful action. When you change your body in some physical, permanent way, you are loudly declaring "This is mine. I can do with it what I will. I can change it to suit my desires, and I can brand it as my own". It's liberating to see your body changed in some way that you have imagined and then acted out on your flesh. It's sensual in its own way, and the pain that often comes with it is a visceral reminder that you're alive, you are embodied, and you are solid. It creates an adrenaline rush of knowing what's about to come. It can be a powerful emotional experience that connects you very deeply with your body.

In addition, for those people who have powerful negative associations with their bodies, tattooing or piercing over the site of negativity can mean a lot. I have scars from self-harm on my hips and legs, and have plans to tattoo over at least some of them as a metaphorical way of reclaiming that territory. Our bodies go through a great deal that leaves us marked in ways that we can't undo. Some of this is by choice, some of it isn't. But the choice to cover or change the marks from the past is a strong statement about who we would like to be in the future.

Tattoos Convey Messages of Identity

Many people view tattoos as "rebellious", "tacky" or "low class". Many of the reasons they're viewed that way is because marginalized groups often use them to assert their autonomy or their belonging in a group. They mark someone as different, as particularly themselves, and as a BODY. We don't like being marked as bodies. We often view it as objectifying. We don't like to be

How Tattoos Impact Self-Identity

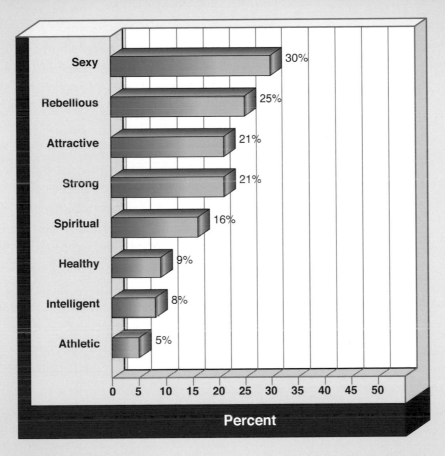

"Compared to not having a tattoo, having a tattoo made me feel . . ."

Category	Percent
Sexy	30%
Rebellious	25%
Attractive	21%
Strong	21%
Spiritual	16%
Healthy	9%
Intelligent	8%
Athletic	5%

Percent

Taken from: Samantha Braverman, "One in Five US Adults Now Has a Tattoo," *The Harris Poll*, no. 22, February 23, 2012. www.harrisinteractive.com.

viewed aesthetically, we prefer to be judged based on our intellect or personality. But the fact is that a major part of our selves is our body. The inherent recognition of this in the act of bodily mutilation or piercing or tattoos is deep, and you can't escape it when you're undergoing the process. You feel more connected to yourself in certain ways. It's one of the reasons that self-harm can be so grounding.

Tattoos also signify a great deal to others: they can tell about our experiences, our emotions, our aesthetic taste, our interests, our values, and our group membership. They use our own bodies to convey messages of our identity, something which is extremely powerful in integrating your body into our identity. In addition, they can signify things to ourselves. They can remind us of our past, of something we care about, of self-care, of good or bad things we've experienced . . . especially for those people whose voices are rarely heard, using your body as a canvas is one of the loudest ways to get a message across.

Some people say that the body is beautiful and shouldn't be tampered with. But for those who are in marginalized groups, they haven't really heard this about their bodies in particular. Their bodies are often viewed as wrong or bad. The few times they do hear these things, their bodies are generally objectified. It can be hugely empowering to make your physical presence different to fit your conception of self. It changes your narrative about self, takes your body away from the societal narrative of beauty, or brands visibly on your body that you have autonomy and are more than a body. Of course these are all comments about tattoos personally chosen: being forced to get a tattoo says the exact opposite of all of this.

It reminds you that you're a body, but also that your body is yours, and that it has its own needs and desires and some autonomy. It's not just an object. Its senses are how you navigate and manage the world, and the act of the tattoo reminds you viscerally of your senses and your physical boundary with the world. The constant reminder of that is an act of asserting yourself into space.

Reminding ourselves of our bodies, of the ways we can control and identify with our bodies, and of how we can present our bodies to others as part of our identity is a big deal.

FIVE

Tattoo Ink–Related Infections: Awareness, Diagnosis, Reporting, and Prevention

Pamela M. LeBlanc, Katherine A. Hollinger, and Karl C. Klontz

> In the following viewpoint Pamela M. LeBlanc, Katherine A. Hollinger, and Karl C. Klontz maintain that tattoo ink has been linked to numerous infections. The authors detail infection outbreaks that have been caused by tattoo ink and also discuss the dangers of tattoo ink contamination. The authors maintain that the Food and Drug Administration (FDA) is working to develop more effective methods for public health problems stemming from tattoo ink. Consumers should take precautions before getting tattoos, the authors assert, and only patronize artists who use sanitary tattooing practices. LeBlanc is a consumer safety officer, Hollinger is an epidemiologist, and Klontz is a medical officer at the FDA.

Tattoos have become increasingly popular in recent years. In the United States, the estimated percentage of adults with one or more tattoos increased from 14% in 2008 to 21% in 2012.[1] The process of tattooing exposes the recipient to risks of infections with various pathogens, some of which are serious and difficult to treat. Historically, the control of tattoo-associated dermatologic infections has focused on ensuring safe tattooing practices and preventing contamination of ink at the tattoo parlors—a regulatory task overseen by state and local authorities.[2] In recent months, however, reported outbreaks of nontuberculous mycobacterial infections associated with contaminated tattoo ink have raised questions about the adequacy of prevention efforts implemented at the tattoo-parlor level alone. The Food and Drug Administration (FDA) is reaching out to health care providers, public health officials, consumers, and the tattoo industry to improve awareness, diagnosis, and reporting (through the MedWatch program) in order to develop more effective measures for tattoo ink–related public health problems.

In late January 2012, the FDA was notified, through MedWatch adverse-event reports,[3] of a cluster of patients in New York who had contracted nontuberculous mycobacterial infections manifested by red papules on the gray-colored areas of recently acquired tattoos. The FDA collaborated with local and state health departments and the Centers for Disease Control and Prevention to investigate the outbreak. Efforts to identify additional cases nationwide revealed that there were other outbreaks of tattoo ink–related nontuberculous mycobacterial infection that were associated with multiple brands of ink, occurred in other states, and involved multiple species of mycobacteria (e.g., chelonae, fortuitum, and abscessus).

Previously published reports of tattoo-related nontuberculous mycobacterial infections suggested that tap water or distilled water used to dilute inks at tattoo parlors was a likely source of contamination.[4] Findings from the recent outbreak investigations, however, suggested that the inks were contaminated before distribution. During the response to the New York outbreak, the outbreak strain of mycobacteria was isolated from an unopened ink container. Thus, contamination could have occurred at various points in the ink-production process—for instance, from unsanitary manufacturing processes or the use of contaminated ingredients such as water, glycerin, or pigments.

Risks Involved in Tattooing

Primary complications that can result from tattooing:

Infection	Unsterile tattooing equipment and needles can transmit infectious diseases, such as HIV, hepatitis, and skin infections caused by *Staphylococcus aureus* ("staph") and other bacteria.
Removal problems	Despite advances in laser technology, removing a tattoo is a painstaking process, usually involving several treatments and considerable expense. Complete removal without scarring may be impossible.
Allergic reactions	Reports of allergic reactions to tattoo pigments have been rare. Occasionally, people may develop an allergic reaction to tattoos they have had for years.
Granulomas	These are nodules that may form around material that the body perceives as foreign, such as particles of tattoo pigment.
Keloid formation	If you are prone to developing keloids—scars that grow beyond normal boundaries—you are at risk of keloid formation from a tattoo.
MRI complications	There have been reports of people with tattoos or permanent makeup who experienced swelling or burning in the affected areas when they underwent magnetic resonance imaging (MRI).

Taken from: "Tattoos and Permanent Makeup: Fact Sheet," US Food and Drug Administration, August 22, 2012. www.fda.gov.

Under the Federal Food, Drug, and Cosmetic Act, tattoo inks are considered to be cosmetics,[5] whereas the pigments used in the inks are color additives that require premarketing approval. This law requires that cosmetics and their ingredients not be adulterated or misbranded, which means, among other things, that they cannot contain poisonous or deleterious substances or unapproved color additives, be manufactured or held in unsanitary conditions,

One health risk associated with tattoos is skin infection from contaminated tattoo ink. The US Food and Drug Administration is exploring ways to prevent contamination to tattoo ink prior to its distribution to shops.

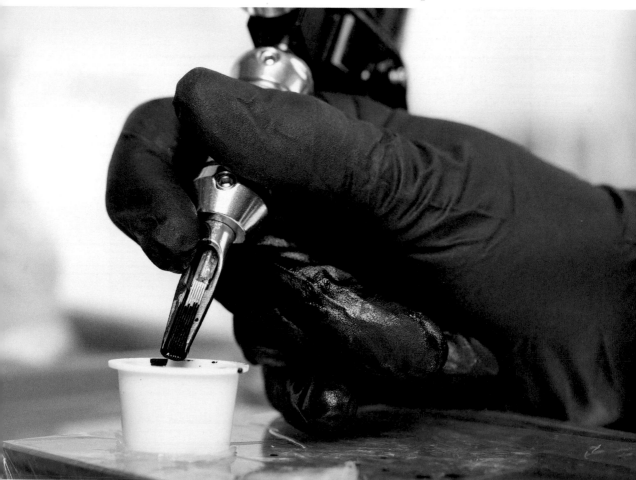

or be falsely labeled. Furthermore, cosmetic manufacturers are supposed to ensure the safety of a product before marketing it.

However, the FDA does not have the authority to require pre-marketing submission of safety data from manufacturers, distributors, or marketers of cosmetic products, with the exception of most color additives (dyes, pigments, or other substances used to impart color). The FDA does have the authority to take other actions to protect the public health. For example, the agency can conduct investigations, request that a manufacturer recall violative products, and issue advisory letters. The agency can also request that the Department of Justice conduct seizures, enjoin a firm or person from manufacturing or distributing products, or file criminal charges against a firm or responsible persons on behalf of the FDA.

Several features of nontuberculous mycobacteria make it particularly important to increase awareness about these types of tattoo ink–related infections. Nontuberculous mycobacterial infections may be difficult to diagnose and treat. Commonly reported symptoms of such infections associated with tattoo ink include lesions consisting of red papules solely in areas where the contaminated ink has been applied. Symptoms can be difficult to recognize, since other conditions (e.g., allergic reactions) may present with similar findings. Recovery of mycobacteria may be challenging, often requiring a skin biopsy, and special culture mediums may be required for diagnosis. Depending on the medium used, it can take up to 6 weeks to identify the organism. Because of these diagnostic challenges, infections may initially be misdiagnosed and patients may receive ineffective treatments. Antibiotic choices are limited by the susceptibility profile of the organism, and prolonged treatment may be necessary to clear the infection. Moreover, complications such as coinfection with pathogens such as methicillin-resistant Staphylococcus aureus may pose a further challenge to a patient's full recovery. Many of the persons affected by the recent tattoo-associated outbreaks of mycobacterial infection who received medical treatment were given macrolide therapy, to which they had a favorable response. Health care providers need to be aware of the symptoms associated with nontuberculous mycobacterial infections from tattoo ink, the challenges involved in diagnosing and treating them, and their own essential role in reporting such cases to MedWatch.

Even if a person receives a tattoo at a tattoo parlor that maintains the highest standards of hygienic practice, there remains a risk of infection from the use of contaminated ink. People who get tattoos must be made aware of this risk and should seek medical attention if lesions consisting of red papules or a diffuse macular rash develop at the tattoo site. Consumers should patronize artists who use sanitary tattooing practices and who can confirm that their inks have undergone a process that eliminates harmful microbial contaminants.

References

1. Braverman S. One in five U.S. adults now has a tattoo. New York: Harris Interactive, 2012 (http://www.harrisinteractive .com/vault/Harris%20Poll%2022%20-Tattoos_2.23.12.pdf).
2. Armstrong ML. Tattooing, body piercing, and permanent cosmetics: a historical and current view of state regulations, with continuing concerns. J Environ Health 2005;67:38–43.
3. Food and Drug Administration. Reporting serious problems to FDA. 2012 (http://www.fda.gov/Safety/MedWatch /HowToReport/default.htm).
4. Drage LA, Ecker PM, Orenstein R, Phillips PK, Edson RS. An outbreak of *Mycobacterium chelonae* infections in tattoos. J Am Acad Dermatol 2010;62:501–6.
5. Food and Drug Administration. Cosmetics: tattoos and permanent makeup. 2010 (http://www.fda.gov/Cosmetics /ProductandIngredientSafety/ProductInformation/ucm108530 .htm).

SIX

Temporary Tattoos May Put You at Risk

US Food and Drug Administration

In the following viewpoint the US Food and Drug Administration (FDA) warns consumers about the dangers of temporary tattoos. Many people view temporary tattoos as harmless, the material asserts, but they do pose potential health risks. The article details reports from consumers of serious reactions from temporary tattoos that range from blisters to lesions and permanent scarring. The FDA highlights black henna in particular, which is often made up of ingredients that are harmful to consumers. The FDA is an agency of the US Department of Health and Human Services that oversees the safety and regulation of food, dietary supplements, drugs, cosmetics, and tobacco products.

Spring break is on the way, or maybe summer vacation. Time to pack your swimsuit, hit the beach, and perhaps indulge in a little harmless fun. What about getting a temporary tattoo to mark the occasion? Who could it hurt to get a temporary tattoo?

Temporary Tattoos Are Not Risk-Free

It could hurt you, if you actually get one. Temporary tattoos typically last from three days to several weeks, depending on the

"FDA Consumer Updates," US Food and Drug Administration, Mach 25, 2013.

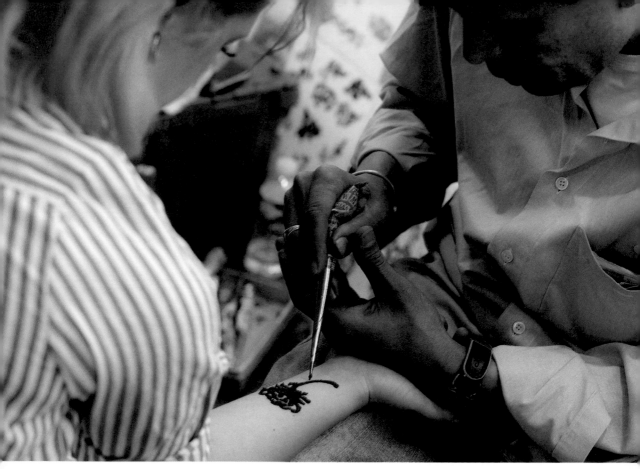

Many health risks are associated with temporary tattoos made with black henna, which, unlike the traditional reddish brown henna, uses harsh chemicals to achieve its dark color.

product used for coloring and the condition of the skin. Unlike permanent tattoos, which are injected into the skin, temporary tattoos marketed as "henna" are applied to the skin's surface.

However, "just because a tattoo is temporary it doesn't mean that it is risk free," says Linda Katz, M.D., M.P.H., director of FDA's [US Food and Drug Administration] Office of Cosmetics and Colors. Some consumers report reactions that may be severe and long outlast the temporary tattoos themselves.

MedWatch, FDA's safety information and adverse event (bad side effects) reporting program, has received reports of serious and long-lasting reactions that consumers had not bargained for after getting temporary tattoos. Reported problems include redness, blisters, raised red weeping lesions, loss of pigmentation, increased sensitivity to sunlight, and even permanent scarring.

Some reactions have led people to seek medical care, including visits to hospital emergency rooms. Reactions may occur immediately after a person gets a temporary tattoo, or even up to two or three weeks later.

The Danger of Black Henna

You may be familiar with henna, a reddish-brown coloring made from a flowering plant that grows in tropical and subtropical regions of Africa and Asia. Since the Bronze Age, people have used dried henna, ground into a paste, to dye skin, hair, fingernails, leather, silk and wool. This decoration—sometimes also known as mehndi—is still used today around the world to decorate the skin in cultural festivals and celebrations.

However, today so-called "black henna" is often used in place of traditional henna. Inks marketed as black henna may be a mix of henna with other ingredients, or may really be hair dye alone. The reason for adding other ingredients is to create a tattoo that is darker and longer lasting, but use of black henna is potentially harmful.

That's because the extra ingredient used to blacken henna is often a coal-tar hair dye containing p-phenylenediamine (PPD), an ingredient that can cause dangerous skin reactions in some people. Sometimes, the artist may use a PPD-containing hair dye alone. Either way, there's no telling who will be affected. By law, PPD is not permitted in cosmetics intended to be applied to the skin.

You may see "black henna" used in places such as temporary tattoo kiosks at beaches, boardwalks, and other holiday destinations, as well as in some ethnic or specialty shops. While states have jurisdiction over professional practices such as tattooing and cosmetology, that oversight differs from state to state. Some states have laws and regulations for temporary tattooing, while others don't. So, depending on where you are, it's possible no one is checking to make sure the artist is following safe practices or even knows what may be harmful to consumers.

Types of Temporary Tattoos

Decal-type (press-on)	An image printed on water-permeable paper is placed ink-side down on the skin. The image is transferred to the skin when the backing is saturated with water.
Airbrush	An artist sprays alcohol-based, cosmetic inks freehand or with a stencil.
Henna (red-to-brown, black, and premixed)	Designs are painted directly on the skin. The paste-like paint is removed hours later, and a rendering of the design is left.
Kits (inkjet or laser printer)	Kit-based tattoos are applied the same way as decal-type temporary tattoos.
Microinjection	Microinjection machines are used to apply colorants into the skin, but not to the depth of typical permanent tattoo processes.

Taken from: "Safety Standards," TM International, 2014. http://tattoomanufacturing.com.

Bad Reactions from Black Henna

A number of consumers have learned the risks the hard way, reporting significant bad reactions shortly after the application of black henna temporary tattoos.

- The parents of a 5-year-old girl reported that she developed severe reddening on her forearm about two weeks after receiving a black henna temporary tattoo. "What we thought would be a little harmless fun ended up becoming more like a nightmare for us," the father says. "My hope is that by telling people about our experience, I can help prevent this from happening to some other unsuspecting kids and parents."

- The mother of a 17-year-old girl agrees. "At first I was a little upset she got the tattoo without telling me," she says. "But when it became red and itchy and later began to blister and the blisters filled with fluid, I was beside myself." She explains that as a nurse, she's used to seeing all manner of injuries, "but when it's your own child, it's pretty scary," she says.
- And another mother, whose teenager had no reaction to red henna tattoos, describes the skin on her daughter's back as looking "the way a burn victim looks, all blistered and raw" after a black henna tattoo was applied there. She says that according to her daughter's doctor, the teenager will have scarring for life.

SEVEN

What to Know Before You Get a Tattoo

Orly Avitzur

In the following viewpoint Orly Avitzur contends that many people get tattoos without exploring the health risks. Avitzur maintains that there are numerous health risks associated with tattoos, and there is no federal regulation of tattooing practices. Because tattoo regulation varies across the country, the author asserts that consumers must take precautions. The author emphasizes the importance of safe inking and offers consumers tips for what to do before getting a tattoo. Avitzur is a neurologist, medical writer, and medical adviser to *Consumer Reports*.

I'm often surprised to hear my patients say that they got their tattoos while they were intoxicated. These confessions usually pour out spontaneously, prompted by anxiety, as I prepare to insert a needle for medical reasons. Getting a tattoo may be exciting, but you shouldn't get drunk and cloud your judgment before you get one.

Permanent tattoos have been growing in popularity (pop star Justin Bieber's tattoos even have their own fan website). Twenty-one percent of all U.S. adults admit to having at least one tattoo, according to a Harris Interactive poll taken this year [2012], up from the 14 percent of Americans who said so in 2008. Adults age 30 to 39 are most likely to have a tattoo (38 percent), and women are slightly more likely than men to have tattoos (23 percent vs. 19 percent).

No longer just the stigmata of sailors, prison inmates, and bik- ers, tattoos have gone mainstream, prompted in part by celebrity body art. Pop star Rihanna, who reportedly has 17, admits she gets

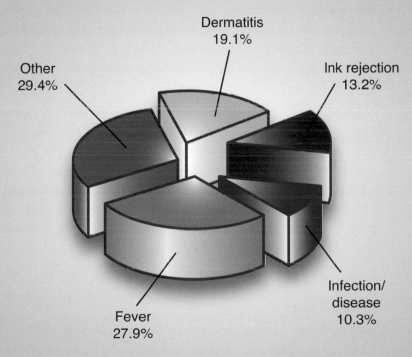

Types of Complications Resulting from Getting Tattooed or Pierced

Dermatitis
19.1%

Ink rejection
13.2%

Other
29.4%

Infection/
disease
10.3%

Fever
27.9%

Note: Based on a sample of 61 people who had experienced complications.

Taken from: Alessia Quaranta et al., "Body Piercing and Tattoos: A Survey on Young Adults' Knowledge of the Risks and Practices in Body Art," *BMC Public Health*, October 7, 2011. www.ncbi.nlm.nih.gov/pmc/articles/PMC3196715.

"tattoo fever" when the impulse strikes. Singers Miley Cyrus and Selena Gomez, actors Johnny Depp, Colin Farrell, Angelina Jolie, and Brad Pitt, along with quite a few athletes have also flaunted their tattoos.

The Health Risks

But as tattooing has spread, so have the associated health risks—skin infections, allergic reactions, and blood-borne diseases. Recently in Rochester, N.Y., 19 patrons of a tattoo parlor were infected with the organism Mycobacterium chelonae, which causes a rash and bumps on the skin; left untreated, the bacteria can spread to the lungs. The tattooing was performed using pre-mixed gray ink, manufactured in Arizona, that had been contaminated before distribution, according to a *New England Journal of Medicine* report. And outbreaks of MRSA (Methicillin-resistant staphylococcus aureus) skin infections from commercially acquired tattoos have also been reported.

State and local authorities oversee tattoo practices, which vary considerably across the country. There is no standard regulation for training or licensing, and virtually no requirements for inspection, record-keeping, or informed consent. Although most states have laws prohibiting minors from getting tattoos, many teens nonetheless find them easy to get.

And almost anyone can put up a tattoo shingle. For example, in New York City, where tattoo parlors are not licensed, a tattooist can get a practitioner's license after simply paying some fees and passing a three-hour infection control course.

Safer Inking

In New York's Westchester and Putnam counties, where I practice, tattoo shops are unregulated, leaving multiple opportunities for health dangers. Because the skin itself is teeming with organisms, if rigorous infection control practices are not used, it can become easily infected when pierced. If equipment or surfaces are improperly sterilized, or if needles are reused, it's possible for viruses such as hepatitis to be transmitted from people who were tattooed earlier.

In addition, blood splatter can contaminate tattoo inks, which are often sold in more economical bulk containers. Sterile, single-use inks are available, but they are more expensive and rarely

Finding a tattoo parlor that practices good hygiene is the best way to avoid tattoo-related health risks. Tattoo artists should always wear gloves, instruments should always be sterilized between clients, and needles should never be reused.

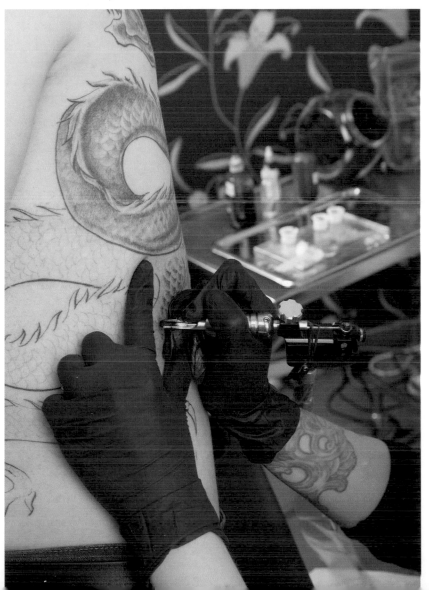

offered. Tattoo inks, which may be chemically complex and contain metals and solvents, are not regulated by the Food and Drug Administration. These inks may consist of azo pigments that not only contain multiple impurities, but are also used in car paint. Many of these pigments are illegal to use in cosmetics in Europe because they can break down into cancer-causing compounds, which may be absorbed into the skin.

If your mind is still set on a new tattoo, be sure to take these precautions.

1. Find a tattoo artist who has single-use, "throw-away" kits that are individually packaged, dated, and sealed and hold disposable needles and tubes. Watch your tattoo artist remove the new needle and tube from its sealed envelope immediately before your session.
2. Make sure that the tattoo parlor is fully licensed (if your state regulates tattoo parlors), and that your tattooist has a great deal of experience, even if that means driving across county lines to find a licensed shop.
3. Make sure the artist wears sterile disposable gloves for each client and use sterile disposable towels, much as you'd expect from your dentist.
4. Watch a procedure first to make sure that unsterile surfaces and equipment are not touched by the tattoo artist once the procedure has begun.
5. Look for telltale signs of sloppy tattoo practices, such as blood splatter, dirty work surfaces, the absence of red "sharps disposal containers," and a lack of infection-control practices.
6. Ask where the ink was manufactured and procured. "It's best if the ink comes from a large manufacturer that has been in business a long time, and even better if the artists have tried the ink on themselves," says Byron Kennedy, M.D., deputy director of health for Monroe County, N.Y., and the lead author of the NEJM story. The contaminated ink in the recent outbreak came from a small retailer, he pointed out.

7. Ask if the inks used are made of nonmetallic organic pigments.

8. Consult a doctor if you see any sign of rash or infection (redness, swelling, or drainage of pus).

EIGHT

Teen Piercing Trends: Earlobe Gauging, Stretching and Body Piercing

Mary Fetzer

> In the following viewpoint Mary Fetzer asserts that body piercing is safe when performed with standard precautions. The author interviews the medical liaison for the Association of Professional Piercers, who offers guidelines for teens to follow before getting pierced. The author provides an overview of the most common piercings among teenagers as well as a new trend called stretching. In addition, Fetzer offers a list of piercing locations on the body that pose the most risk to consumers and advises teens to avoid piercing these body parts. Fetzer is a marketing consultant and freelance writer located in central Pennsylvania.

When done properly, piercing is safe. Elayne Angel is the author of *The Piercing Bible: The Definitive Guide to Safe Body Piercing* and the Medical Liaison for the Association of Professional Piercers (APP) and recommends following standard safety precautions for a safe piercing experience:

- the piercing should be done in a hygienic facility by a trained, experienced worker

*Ear stretching is a trendy body modification, but it can
be difficult to reverse if proper care isn't taken during the
stretching process or if the earlobe is stretched too much.*

- sterile, disposable equipment should be used
- jewelry of the correct material, size, and style should be inserted
- proper aftercare instructions should be followed

Tongue and Nose Piercings in Teens

Tongue and nose piercings are pretty common among today's
teens. And while many parents are over the shock factor, they
still worry that tongue and nose piercings are unsanitary.

Contrary to popular belief, Angel says oral piercings are not especially prone to infection. The mouth and nose have tremendous defensive strategies. In fact, the mouth is one of the fastest healing sites in the body. A tongue piercing can heal in six-to-eight weeks, says Angel, while a navel piercing can take up to nine months to heal.

A New Trend—Stretching

Have you seen earlobe piercings that are large enough to look through? . . . It's sometimes referred to as gauging, but "piercers loathe the term gauging," says Angel. "We call it stretching. And the jewelry worn in stretched pierces—plugs, eyelets, talons, and other jewelry designs—should never be called gauges."

Whatever the name, it's an unsettling trend. What motivates a person to do this? Is it dangerous? Can it be undone?

Why Stretch Your Ear?

Andrew B. has always marched to the beat of a different drummer, but his decision to stretch his earlobes wasn't about nonconformity or rebellion. "I saw a guy with [stretching] at a pizza shop and thought it was pretty cool," says Andrew.

Andrew's parents weren't thrilled with his decision to put giant holes in his earlobes, but "I told them it was no different than my mom copying a hairstyle she liked," says Andrew.

How Stretching Is Done

For stretching, Angel recommends going up no more than one size at a time. "You must allow sufficient time between each enlargement," Angel says, "for the tissue to fully regain its suppleness and integrity." Angel explains that skin is resilient if it's not abused.

When an individual becomes impatient and tries to force the piercing, the consequences can be severe. "Overstretching can result in a buildup of scar tissue and reduction of flexibility," warns

Angel. This can make it difficult to stretch in the future or to shrink back to normal.

How Teens Sneak Stretching by Parents

It's this slow speed of stretching that also lets teens sneak the process right by their parents. One mother said she had no idea her son was stretching his earlobes until it was too late. "I was fine with his pierced ears," she says, "and I just thought he was wearing bigger and stranger earrings. I didn't know it was a means to this end."

So, how do you undo it?

Repairing a Stretched or Gauged Ear

When stretching is done properly, the channel could shrink down to leave a minimal mark when jewelry is removed, says Angel. Stretches over one-half inch, however, will probably not return to a normal appearance. In order to be rid of the void, plastic surgery may be necessary.

Facial plastic surgeon D.J. Verret, MD, repairs earlobe stretchings on a regular basis. "The biggest age group coming for repair," says Verret, "are high school and college graduates entering the job market."

According to Dr. Verret, the success of the repair process is dependent on how much earlobe skin is left. Verret compares cases with less skin to repairs for people born without earlobes or those who have lost their earlobes due to trauma.

Please Don't Pierce That!

Angel is a strong advocate for expression through piercing, but there are some piercings that even she refuses to perform. Steer your teen away from these risky piercings:

- Face: eyelid, lip surface, chin, horizontal (transverse) tongue, cheek, between the cheek and gum line, under the tongue, uvula (at the back of the throat)

Millennials Are Most Likely to Have Body Piercings

Percent of people who have a piercing somewhere other than an earlobe, by generation

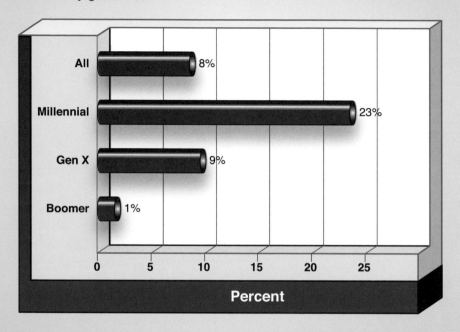

Taken from: "Millennials: A Portrait of Generation Next," Pew Research Center, February 2010. http://pewsocialtrends.org.

- Torso: outie navel, small or inverted nipples, under the collarbone
- Genitals: deep clitoral shaft (the Isabella), female urethra opening (the Princess Albertina), deep penile shaft, and transcrotal
- Other body parts not to pierce: anus, between fingers and toes or anywhere on the hands and feet, close to skin's surface through a small pinch of tissue, behind bone or tendon

The Bottom Line

Angel, who has performed over 40,000 piercings in her professional career, believes piercing is safe when both the piercer and pierce are educated about the process. Check out safepiercing.org for more information.

NINE

Teens Should Not Get Trendy Body Piercings

Leah S.

In the following viewpoint a young woman named Leah S. argues that teenagers should not pursue body modification just to follow the latest trends. While body modification is growing in popularity, the author advises teenagers against getting body piercings and tattoos that will quickly go out of fashion. While teens may want to use tattoos or body piercings to express their personal style, she believes they should think twice before making that decision. Leah S. is a contributor to *Teen Ink*, a national teen magazine, book series, and website.

Throughout the past years, body modification has become more popular and accepted within society. The most common, and most widely accepted, form of body modification is the ear piercing. While an ear piercing may seem bland or generic, many people have found different ways to make the piercing their own. The Gauge, the Stud, and the Cartilage are the three most common and accepted forms of ear piercings. The classification of ear piercings is vital to anyone who ever needs to sort out the type of people they meet.

Percentage of Adults with Ear, Face, and Body Piercings

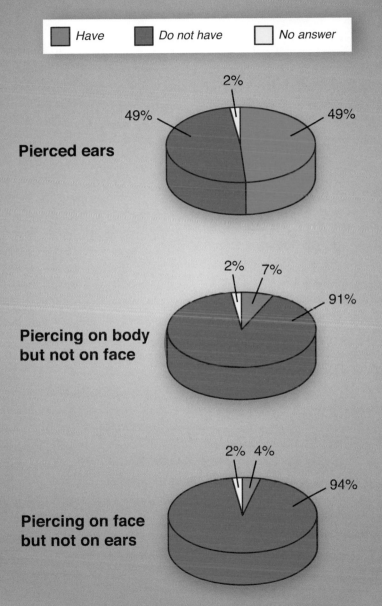

Have   Do not have   No answer

Pierced ears
2%
49%
49%

Piercing on body but not on face
2%   7%
91%

Piercing on face but not on ears
2%   4%
94%

Taken from: Samantha Braverman, "One in Five US Adults Now Has a Tattoo," *The Harris Poll*, no. 22, February 23, 2012. www.harrisinteractive.com.

A young woman displays her neck tattoos and "gauge" style of ear piercing. Teens should use caution before modifying their bodies; trendy modifications can soon go out of style.

The Gauge

Growing in popularity, gauging is the practice of stretching one's ear out by increasing the size of his or her earring. These piercings, which typically have a horrendous stench, have become popular partly because of the recent change in music trends. Teens listening to hardcore rock or screamo bands such as: The Devil Wears Prada, IWrestledABearOnce, and A Day To Remember sport gauges. Gauges range in size, beginning at eighteen gauge and usually stopping around double zero. Someone bearing a double zero gauge can fit a wine cork through their extremely elastic earlobe. Many teens participating in gauging their ears usually have other body modifications or piercings: the septum, bridge, snakebites, spider bites, Monroe's, et cetera. While hardcore music may influence teens to show their unique style, the Gauge is just another fad that will quickly go out of fashion.

The Stud

While the Stud is the most popular piercing, there are a variety of classifications inside of this simple piercing. First, there are the trashy parents who pierce their children's ears directly after the child exits the parent's womb. Besides the newborns with their ears pierced, there are the girls hitting puberty who have finally gained the privilege of getting a hole in their ear. What a pleasant way to start womanhood: someone hurting a young girl for the sake of beauty! Next, there are the women who have never had the courage to deliberately hurt themselves due to low pain tolerance or some other pathetic excuse. But these women have decided, "Hey! Maybe something hanging from my ear will look fantastic with my new outfit". My personal favorites are the guys who think that having a stud piercing actually make themselves studs. The males decked out at bars sporting gelled up hair, popped collars, loud rap music, and their flashy "bling" on their ears easily top off the category of the stud.

The Cartilage

The Cartilage is the perfect final touch for the bleach blonde Barbie wannabes. Although this piercing was trendy, it has now turned into a discrete tramp stamp. A few teens may be seen with this piercing because extra holes in their ears are the cool thing to do, but they are unaware of the meaning behind their cartilage piercing. The Cartilage, better known as Barbie, is usually found at Planet Beach getting a flawless orange glow to her skin tone. College students who have their cartilage pierced usually have, or plan to have, other, more provocative forms of body art. The Cartilage is typically found out at a local club socializing with the male Stud, who is desperately attempting to buy the Cartilage some overly fruity adult beverage.

There is no purpose behind the Gauge, the Stud, or the Cartilage except for the sake of pain, stupidity, or lack of trendiness. While all three categories have different styles, the one similarity is that there is no reason to pay money to pierce a hole in someone's ear, let alone increase the size of the hole intentionally. And, the next time you find yourself contemplating acquiring a piercing, be sure to reflect upon the types of ear piercings and how "trendy" that hole in your ear will appear.

TEN

Teens Should Be Able to Get Tattoos

Silvia Cardona-Tapia

> In the following viewpoint Silvia Cardona-Tapia argues that teenagers should have the right to get tattoos. She details the motivations for getting a tattoo and asserts that tattoos have the power to keep memories alive. Responsible teenagers should be able to express themselves by getting tattoos, the author argues, and states that require teenagers to wait until they are eighteen to get tattooed infringe upon their right to have control over their own bodies. Cardona-Tapia believes that the minimum age to get a tattoo should be thirteen, with a parent's consent. At the time this viewpoint was written, Cardona-Tapia was a staff writer at the *Mosaic*, the blog of the Mosaic San Jose High School Journalism Workshop.

I believe one's own uniqueness can be expressed through tattoos. Parents have to learn how to give their teens a chance and let them have tattoos. If the parents don't let them, the teens will go behind their backs.

I have many friends with tattoos and they are underage. In California, the legal age for getting a tattoo is 18. My friends should not be looked at in the wrong way.

They have a right to their own bodies and if they feel like they want to go get a tattoo, they should have the right to do so.

Some of the reasons that most teens get tattoos include the desire for social bonding with others, to show the respect to their loved one, or to honor someone they love.

Gilbert Macheca was 13 when the friend of a friend tattooed the words, "One Love" on the top of each of his hands reflecting

A sign on the door to a tattoo parlor warns "No Minors." Most states require a person to be eighteen or to have parental consent to get a tattoo.

his passion for rapping and reggae music. He had it done without asking his parents first.

"My mom was disappointed when she saw my hands, but then she realized it was my body," said Macheca, who is now 17. "She got over it after a few days."

Tattoos Keep Memories Alive

It's not as if minors with tattoos are running around with the bloody needles that were used to create their tattoos.

I'm not saying that California should let babies get tattoos. But waiting until 18 is too difficult for a lot of kids. The minimum age should be 13 with a parent's consent form.

Tattoos can keep memories alive. For example, some teens show their feelings to their loved ones by getting tattoos of their names or getting a tattoo that reminds them of the one they love or lost.

When I turned 15 two years ago, I wanted a tattoo in Old English of the two most important women in my life, my older sister Pamela and my mother Leticia, who raised me in Mexico and in Oakland. My mother worked day and night to keep food on the table, a house, and for me to have everything I needed.

Three months ago a boy I loved died from a seizure and I wanted to get a tattoo that reminded me of him. I want the image of an angel over the Earth.

I didn't get the tattoos because I decided I can wait a few months until I'm legal age and do it without permission. But some teens can't help their emotions and will get them done illegally.

I admit that a lot of teens don't have anything important to say with a tattoo. They just want tattoos to anger their parents or rebel against society.

"I just wanted to get one. I don't regret it because I've wanted one for a long time," said Dajaror Bryson, who got a friend to tattoo her astrological sign, Capricorn, on her wrist at age 16.

Even though hers might seem like a silly tattoo, silly tattoos reflect memories, too. I have a friend who proposed a pact where everyone in our group would get a tattoo of their astrological sign

State Laws on Tattooing of Minors

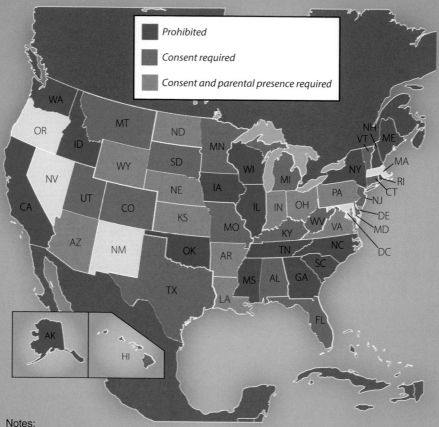

Legend:
- Prohibited
- Consent required
- Consent and parental presence required

Notes:
Georgia, Illinois, and Wisconsin: The prohibition does not apply when the tattooing is performed by a physician or licensed technician under a physician's supervision.
Idaho: Prohibition for those under 14, consent required for ages 14–18.
Iowa: Prohibition applies only to unmarried minors.
South Carolina: Prohibition for those under 18, consent required for ages 18–21.
Tennessee: Prohibition for those under 16, consent required for ages 16–18.
Tennessee and Texas: Tattooing of minors is allowed only for covering up an existing tattoo.

Taken from: "Tattoos and Body Piercings for Minors," National Conference of State Legislatures, May 2013. www.ncsl.org.

before we all head to college. I think it's a great pact because that shows how much we love each other.

I can wait until I'm 18, but I shouldn't have to and neither should other responsible teenagers.

ELEVEN

Inked and Regretful: Removing Tattoos

US Food and Drug Administration

> In the following viewpoint the US Food and Drug Administration (FDA) maintains that the number of people getting tattoo removal is on the rise. The FDA warns consumers to be careful before seeking tattoo removal treatment. The article describes various methods for removing tattoos and highlights laser removal treatment, which is the most commonly used procedure and is approved by the FDA. However, even laser tattoo removal is not guaranteed, the viewpoint maintains, and it may not be possible to completely remove the tattoo or avoid scarring. The FDA is an agency of the US Department of Health and Human Services that oversees the safety and regulation of food, dietary supplements, drugs, cosmetics, and tobacco products.

That tattoo on your arm of a former flame—the one that seemed like a great idea years ago—is kind of embarrassing today. And your spouse is not too crazy about it either.

You may not know that FDA [US Food and Drug Administration] considers the inks used in tattoos to be cosmetics, and the

"Inked and Regretful: Removing Tattoos," FDA Consumer Updates, US Food and Drug Administration, January 30, 2013.

agency takes action to protect consumers when safety issues arise related to the inks.

At the other end of the tattoo process, FDA also regulates laser devices used to remove tattoos.

Main Reasons for Tattoo Removal

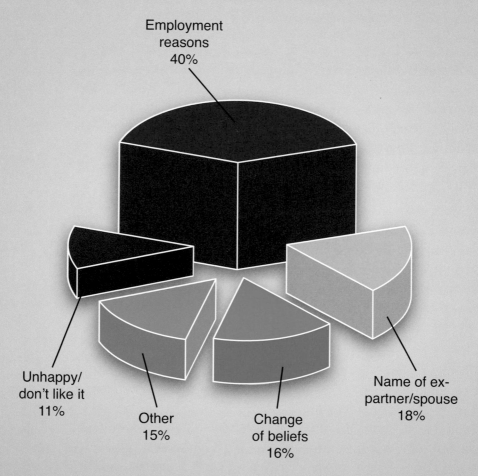

Employment reasons 40%

Name of ex-partner/spouse 18%

Change of beliefs 16%

Other 15%

Unhappy/ don't like it 11%

Note: Survey data from over 700 participants who made appointments for in-office laser tattoo removal. Patients were asked to indicate their main reason for initiating the treatment.

Taken from: "Study: Tattoo Removal Climbs 32% in Competitive Job Market," *Patient's Guide* (Blog), May 23, 2012. www.patientsguide.com.

FDA has cleared for marketing several types of lasers as light-based, prescription devices for tattoo lightening or removal. A Massachusetts company recently received FDA clearance to market its laser workstation for the removal of tattoos and benign skin lesions.

According to a poll conducted in January 2012 by pollster Harris Interactive, 1 in 8 (14%) of the 21% of American adults who have tattoos regret getting one. And the American Society for Dermatologic Surgery (ASDS) reports that in 2011, its doctors performed nearly 100,000 tattoo removal procedures, up from the 86,000 performed in 2010.

A Painstaking Process

Unfortunately, removing a tattoo is not as simple as changing your mind.

Artists create tattoos by using an electrically powered machine that moves a needle up and down to inject ink into the skin, penetrating the epidermis, or outer layer, and depositing a drop of ink into the dermis, the second layer. The cells of the dermis are more stable compared with those of the epidermis, so the ink will mostly stay in place for a person's lifetime. Tattoos are meant to be permanent.

An effective and safe way to remove tattoos is through laser surgery, performed by a dermatologist who specializes in tattoo removal, says FDA's Mehmet Kosoglu, Ph.D., who reviews applications for marketing clearances of laser devices.

"Laser" stands for Light Amplification by Stimulated Emission of Radiation. Kosoglu says that pulsed lasers, which emit concentrated light energy in short bursts, or pulses, have been used to remove tattoos for more than 20 years.

However, it can be a painstaking process. "Complete removal, with no scarring, is sometimes not possible," Kosoglu notes.

FDA clearance means this method for removing tattoos complies with agency requirements for safety and effectiveness, according to FDA dermatologist Markham Luke, M.D. Other methods include dermabrasion—actually "sanding" away the top layer of

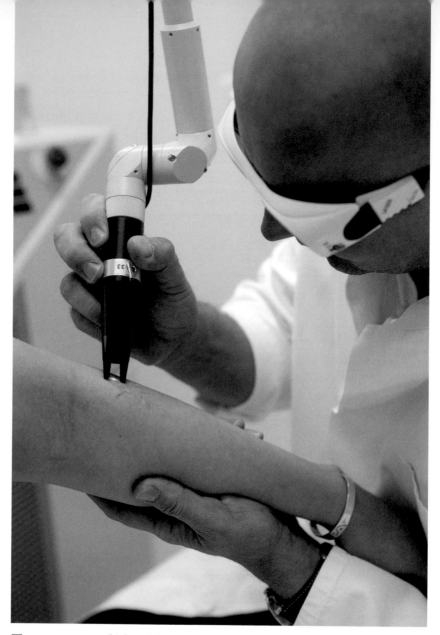

*Tattoo removal should be done only by a licensed derma-
tologist performing laser surgery. Even then, there is no
guarantee that a tattoo will be fully removed.*

skin—and excision—cutting away the area of the tattoo and then
sewing the skin back together.

There are also do-it-yourself tattoo removal ointments and
creams that you can buy online. "FDA has not approved them,

and is not aware of any clinical evidence that they work," says Luke. In addition, Luke says that tattoo removal ointments and creams may cause unexpected reactions, such as rashes, burning, scarring, or changes in skin pigmentation in the process.

Complete Removal Is Not Always Possible

With laser removal, pulses of high-intensity laser energy pass through the epidermis and are selectively absorbed by the tattoo pigment. The laser breaks the pigment into smaller particles, which may be metabolized or excreted by the body, or transported to and stored in lymph nodes or other tissues, Kosoglu explains.

The type of laser used to remove a tattoo depends on the tattoo's pigment colors, he adds. Because every color of ink absorbs different wavelengths of light, multi-colored tattoos may require the use of multiple lasers. Lighter colors such as green, red, and yellow are the hardest colors to remove, while blue and black are the easiest.

"That depends on a person's pain threshold," Kosoglu says. Some people compare the sensation of laser removal to being spattered with drops of hot bacon grease or snapping a thin rubber band against the skin. A trained dermatologist will be able to adjust the treatment to the patient's comfort level.

Multiple Treatments Are Required

Generally speaking, just one laser treatment won't do the trick. According to the American Academy of Dermatology, the procedure requires multiple treatments (typically six to 10) depending on a tattoo's size and colors, and requires a few weeks of healing time between procedures. Some side effects may include pinpoint bleeding, redness, or soreness, none of which should last for long.

Luke says that these laser devices are cleared for use by, or under the supervision of, a health care professional. The removal procedure requires using the correct type of laser, understanding the reaction of tissue to laser, and knowing how to treat the area after the procedure.

"If you have any concerns about having a tattoo removed, it's a good idea to consult your dermatologist, who is knowledgeable about laser treatments," Luke concludes.

TWELVE

Tattoos Represent Modern-Day Social Branding

Reef Karim

> In the following viewpoint Reef Karim maintains that tattoos have become trendier in the last twenty-five years. As tattoos have become more acceptable in society, the author contends, they are now considered body art and a form of self-expression. He explores the motivations behind why people choose to get tattoos, as well as the emotional response at the sight of tattoos. The author believes society is moving toward a trend of communication via tattoos, and that body ink has become a modern form of social branding. Karim is the founder and director of the Control Center in Beverly Hills, California, and an assistant clinical professor at the University of California, Los Angeles.

Body art, body bling, self-graffiti, walking billboards, fashionable ink accessories. . . . Each of these expressions depict the physical nature of the tattoo. What's often NOT discussed, however, is the emotional side of tattoos.

I vividly remember the first time I saw a "tramp stamp." A woman was reaching for something in the front row of a large auditorium and a few rows of men and women witnessed her

"Hmmm. . . . decisions, decisions!," cartoon by -Chris Taylor- Roy, www.CartoonStock.com. Copyright © -Chris Taylor- Roy. Reproduction rights obtainable from www.CartoonStock.com.

walking artistry. Everyone had a reaction. And once she left the room, we all talked about it. It was like group therapy.

The responses ranged from "She's definitely a party girl, probably drinks a lot, has a lot of sex and a rough childhood," to "She's probably really creative, edgy, a leader and an independent thinker." Some liked her more, some liked her less and many guys were more interested in her because of the tattoo. Whatever the response, we were all intrigued, and each of us conjured up our own personal version of her story—all from the sight of a well-placed tattoo.

In those days, tattoos were still controversial. Now, they're more accepted than ever. You could even call them "trendy." In the nightlife scene, tattoo artists are rapidly becoming a popular career choice. Sooner or later, we're going to see a leather-clad, tattoo-sleeved, multi-pierced guy named Rocko at our kid's career fair standing next to the "Be a DJ" booth. Although tattoos have been around for more than 5,000 years (Egyptians used tattoos to differentiate peasants from slaves and social branding has been around a long time), ink art has really exploded in the last 25 years.

Tattoos Have Stories

Is it social branding?

Tattoos are a conversation starter. Either there's a story attached or a "skin"-showing session or an emotional response derived from the sight of ink art. And the emotional response from the sight of tattoos leads to a modern-day version of social branding.

"He must be tough."

"She's probably easy."

"He'll never get a corporate job."

"She just wants to drink vodka tonics and dance on a speaker."

Of course there are variables. In my opinion, the older you are, the less chance you'll be forgiving of tattoos. Neck and face tattoos are usually not as well-received as other locations no matter what your age (sorry, Big Mike). Where you put the tattoo, how may tattoos you have, what the tattoo is and the size of the tattoos all help shape the emotional response of the viewer. And that observer could be anyone from a potential boss, a family member or a date.

You're incredibly naïve or in total denial if you think your tattoos aren't going to have a significant positive or negative influence on people who don't know you well.

Reasons for Tattoos Vary

People get tattoos for many reasons: for attention, self-expression, artistic freedom, rebellion, a visual display of a personal narrative, reminders of spiritual/cultural traditions, sexual motivation, addiction, identification with a group or even drunken impulsiveness (which is why many tattoo parlors are open late).

And now, according to some research studies, 15–38 percent of Americans have some type of long-term body art. What was once considered self-mutilatory behavior and a psychiatric problem has now become almost normative behavior.

Some people mark themselves for life to remind them of past family members or ancient sayings or religious scriptures or names of their current family/love interest. Other people use tattoos to enhance their sexual prowess or feed their exhibitionist side, and many people use tattoos to visually promote their identity and/or group affiliation. "I stand for . . ."

Tattoos are a form of self-expression and, whether intentional or not, elicit an emotional response from those who view them.

Johnny Depp said, "My body is my journal and my tattoos are my story." Tattoos can visually reveal more about you or distract people from getting to know the real you. Some people hide behind their tattoos.

Research on tattoos reveals some interesting findings:

- Adults with tattoos have been shown to be more sexually active than controls without tattoos.
- People with tattoos have been shown to be more likely to engage in . . . higher risk behaviors.
- Women who get tattoos are more than twice as likely to get them removed as men.
- In studying first impressions of people that have tattoos, researchers have found that avatars (neutral) with tattoos and other body modifications were rated as more likely to be thrill and adventure seekers, to have a higher number of previous sexual partners, and to be less inhibited than non-tattooed avatars. This study looked at general stigma associated with people sporting tattoos.
- And another study showed both men and women had higher body appreciation, higher self-esteem and lower anxiety right after getting new tattoos. Surprisingly, three weeks later men continued to have less anxiety but women had a sharp increase in anxiety that may be associated with concerns about body image.

And I've personally seen tattoo markings used as an endorphin release and substitute for addictive behavior. An individual addicted to pills was able to stop popping pills but then subsequently became addicted to getting body ink.

So what does this mean?

Tattoos Are a Form of Self-Expression

Our current society craves individuality and self-expression. And now many people wear their artistic expression. We are having more trouble communicating with each other than ever before, as electronic communication will never replace face-to-face human contact. So, it's not surprising that there's a growing trend toward communication via body ink. We don't have to talk, we just have to look.

Our bodies have become the refrigerator magnets of quotes, sayings and reminders.

Whether you like it or not, tattoos are growing in popularity. The long-term fear of being "marked for life" is being tempered by tattoo removal technology and people getting used to seeing tattoos.

Personally, I chose not to have a tattoo (henna tattoos don't count) because the beauty of life is that it's unexpected and we change with our experiences. What we stand for and believe in at 18 is very different than 35 or 60. If we stood for one thing in life and it never changed, then we could all have "life script" tattoos (and face boredom on a regular basis).

But we do grow and change. I appreciate the artistry of tattoos but also enjoy the mystery of learning about someone without being "visually influenced" to have a response. We all judge, and first impressions probably carry more weight than they should. Whatever your feelings are about tattoos, one thing is for sure: There's definitely more than meets the eye.

THIRTEEN

Job Discrimination Based on Body Modification Is Outdated

Elise Martorano

> In the following viewpoint Elise Martorano argues that employers that ban visible body piercings and tattoos are subscribing to outdated stereotypes about body modification. The author contends that many employers equate body modification with a dangerous or counterculture image. This couldn't be further from the truth, the author maintains, as people from varying cultures and socio-economic backgrounds have body piercings and tattoos. Employers should hire based on merit, Martorano asserts, and not discriminate against candidates with body modification. Martorano is a columnist for the *Massachusetts Daily Collegian*.

I can't even begin to estimate how many jobs I've applied to whose dress codes included a phrase like, "No visible tattoos or piercings." This mandate always rubbed me the wrong way for several reasons, but I think the most important reason is the perceived difference between a visible tattoo and a non-visible tattoo.

Employers want to put a face on their company that inspires trust and confidence in its clients. Fair enough. But what is it

Percentage of Tattooed Workers by Industry

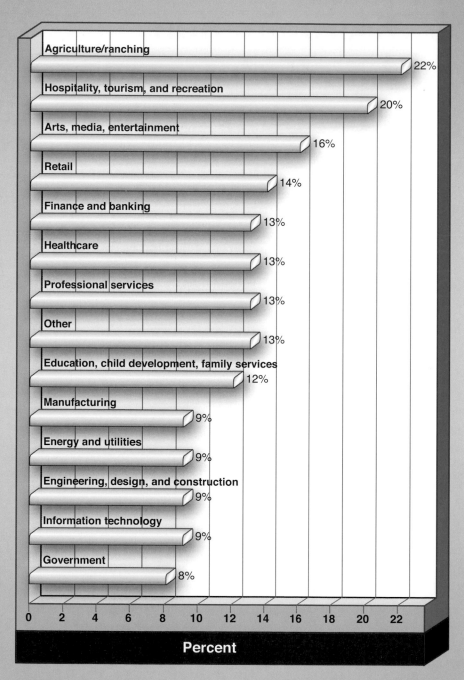

Agriculture/ranching — 22%
Hospitality, tourism, and recreation — 20%
Arts, media, entertainment — 16%
Retail — 14%
Finance and banking — 13%
Healthcare — 13%
Professional services — 13%
Other — 13%
Education, child development, family services — 12%
Manufacturing — 9%
Energy and utilities — 9%
Engineering, design, and construction — 9%
Information technology — 9%
Government — 8%

0 2 4 6 8 10 12 14 16 18 20 22

Percent

about a pierced or tattooed face that causes people to view the company in a negative light? The answer to this question is so outdated it's embarrassing. We typically associate people who have visible body modifications with criminals, plain and simple.

We associate tattooed necks with prison inmates, tattooed biceps with motorcycle gangs, pierced lips with bullies and stretched ears with high school dropouts. This concept is, in itself, inherently flawed for several reasons.

The first reason is that these images of "dangerous people"—people who are intimidating, rude and unintelligent—are highly caricatured and for the most part, outdated. Fear of groups like this, largely representative of underprivileged demographics and also of counterculture movements, has been exaggerated by (mostly white, middle-class) cultural paranoia.

Mainstream Ideas of Professionalism

This paranoia can be extended to countless other ways people express themselves through their bodies: Hair colors and styles, fashion, use of makeup and even women's decisions to shave their body hair. Mainstream society is terrified of people who deviate from the social conventions of what people should look like, and, more relevantly, what professionals should look like.

Although body modifications like this may once have been more or less specific to these groups of people, they aren't anymore. Today, the pierced and tattooed "demographic" is no longer just a demographic. Those who choose to alter their bodies in these ways are represented by countless careers, personalities, cultures, social circles and socioeconomic backgrounds. Body modifications are no longer indicative of the stigmatized pseudo-criminal, if they ever were in the first place.

So how does our perception of individuals with these modifications change when the tattoos or piercings are not visible? Consider two potential employees with equal merit. One enters a job interview with a pierced nose (clearly visible). Another enters the interview with pierced genitals (obviously not visible). In a conservative environment, the potential employee with the genital piercing will, in all likeliness, be far better off. This is because the potential employer cannot see it and is therefore not confronted with the confusing paradigm of a qualified individual with a body modification. Note the sarcasm.

Challenges to Ideas of Equality

If we want to extrapolate this metaphor into a slightly more sinister context, here's another example. Imagine an establishment that does not hire homosexuals, although employees are never asked about it in their interviews. Two potential employees are interviewed. Both are homosexual. The first makes no indication of it, and is hired. The second, on the other hand, is spotted holding the hand of their partner before the interview. This second person, given the company's policy, is not hired.

But what is the fundamental difference between these two individuals? Nothing. Obviously this metaphor is not airtight, especially given the considerably more devastating social discrimination and aggression that homosexuals have experienced and still are experiencing, compared to individuals with body modifications. But you get my point.

In a perhaps outdated practice, many employees are required to cover up tattoos while in the workplace.

Employers, and the general public, do not want to confront the conflicting cultural archetypes that our society has constructed, which cause us to look at people and judge them based on their appearance or demeanor. The concept of a lawyer, a teacher or a salesperson with stretched ears or tattooed knuckles conflicts with how we categorize our conceptions of people.

We love to put groups in Venn diagrams: In this instance, professionals on one side, people with body modifications in the other, a blank space in the middle. It is very difficult for us to rid ourselves of the paranoid misconceptions of past generations. But we must ask ourselves what the purposes of these misconceptions are. What do we stand to gain by continuing to allow ourselves and others to discriminate on the basis of physical appearance (and furthermore, by nationality, sexuality, gender or any other factor that is a common basis for discrimination)? We inhibit ourselves by inhibiting our understanding of other people—we prevent ourselves from learning about and benefitting from the unique perspectives of those who are different from us.

What You Should Know About Body Piercing and Tattoos

Facts About Body Piercing and Tattoos

- In 2013 the *Journal of Drugs in Dermatology* reported that 45 million Americans had a tattoo.
- According to *SFGate*, the higher the education level, the less likely it is an individual will have tattoos. Just 3 percent of PhD holders have tattoos, while 10 percent of those with a bachelor's degree have them; for associate's degree holders the number climbs to 19 percent.
- *SFGate* reports that some regions of the United States are more tattoo-inclined than others. In the Rocky Mountain region, consisting of the states of Idaho, Montana, Wyoming, Nevada, Utah, Colorado, Arizona, and New Mexico, 16 percent of the population has tattoos—more than any other region. On the other end of the spectrum, in the region encompassing the states of Oklahoma, Texas, Arkansas, and Louisiana, only 8 percent of the population has tattoos.
- According to a 2012 Harris Interactive poll, Hispanics reported having tattoos most often, with 30 percent having one or more tattoos, while only 21 percent of black respondents and 20 percent of white respondents have tattoos.
- The same survey reports that 22 percent of Democrats said they have tattoos, while only 17 percent of Republicans have them.

- Among those under the age of thirty, 35 percent of women versus only 11 percent of men have a body piercing somewhere besides the ears, according to the Pew Research Center.
- The Pew Research Center reports that 18 percent of individuals under age thirty with tattoos have six or more of them. Among those age thirty and up with tattoos, only 9 percent have six or more.
- *Smithsonian* magazine reports that the oldest example of humans' use of tattoos dates from more than five thousand years ago, as exhibited in the Iceman, whose mummified body was found in 1991 in the Alps near the Italian-Austrian border.
- Before this discovery, according to *Smithsonian*, ancient Egypt provided the earliest evidence of tattooing, which was practiced only on women during the Egyptian dynastic period.

Attitudes and Behaviors

- The *Journal of Sexual Medicine* finds that adults with body piercings and tattoos who are between the ages of twenty and thirty-five are four times less likely to practice religion than those without. They are also twice as likely as their unmodified peers to have had early sexual experiences.
- In the same study, it was found that the sample of pierced or tattooed young adults showed no statistical difference from their peers concerning sexual orientation, sexual preference, history of sexual abuse, or risky sexual behaviors.
- Nonetheless, according to a 2012 Harris Interactive survey, 24 percent of adults believe that people with tattoos are more likely to engage in deviant behavior, and 50 percent believe that tattooed individuals are more rebellious.
- In a survey of British residents, the journal *Body Image* found that right after getting a tattoo, individuals feel significantly lower appearance anxiety and dissatisfaction.
- The same study found that men and women behave differently regarding their social physique anxiety. While women's

anxiety goes up significantly three weeks after getting a tattoo, men's goes down.

- *Body Image* also found that tattooed individuals are significantly less satisfied with their new tattoos three weeks after getting them.
- *SFGate* reports that education level makes a difference in an individual's perception of tattoos. Only 38 percent of high school graduates found tattoos objectionable, versus 55 percent of PhD holders.
- For body piercings, there was no significant disagreement, according to *SFGate*; regardless of education level, a little more than half of the respondents found body piercings inappropriate in the workplace.
- The Pew Research Center found that for liberals under thirty, 43 percent have tattoos, while those who identify as conservatives have tattoos only 32 percent of the time.
- According to the *Huffington Post*, 19 percent of British vacationers aged eighteen to twenty-five have chosen to get a tattoo while on vacation abroad. Of those, 67 percent regretted the choice.

Body Piercing and Tattoos in the Workplace
- *SFGate* reports that, in a sample of nearly 2,700 people, 12 percent of the survey respondents said they had a tattoo that was visible to their coworkers at their place of work.
- The same study found that only 3 percent had a body piercing other than an earring visible to their coworkers.
- According to *SFGate*, 76 percent of respondents believe that having a tattoo or body piercing can be a deal breaker in the hiring process.
- The same source states that 42 percent believe that tattoos are inappropriate at work, and 55 percent find body piercings objectionable in the work environment.
- Despite these figures, *SFGate* reports that only 4 percent of those with tattoos or piercings have experienced discrimination on the basis of their body modifications.

- CareerBuilder reports that 37 percent of hiring managers would be less likely to promote an employee with piercings, and 31 percent would be less likely to offer a promotion to an employee with visible tattoos.

Facts About the Removal of Tattoos

- The *Journal of Drugs in Dermatology* reports that the majority of people who have chosen to get tattoos (83 percent) are satisfied with their decision. However, 17 percent of them consider tattoo removal and 6 percent actually get their tattoos removed.
- The *Journal of Drugs in Dermatology* found that women are twice as likely to get their tattoos removed as men.
- According to LiveScience, getting a tattoo removed will usually cost ten to twenty times as much as the original cost of the tattoo.
- LiveScience reports that laser treatment does not remove all tattoos equally. Factors that affect tattoo removal are the tattoo's depth and the chemical composition and color of its ink. Laser treatment removes black, red, dark orange, and dark blue tattoos more easily, while green, purple, brown, light orange, and light blue tattoos often require more laser treatment removal sessions.
- The International Association for Physicians in Aesthetic Medicine (IAPAM) reports that the average cost of a fifteen-minute tattoo removal treatment is about $200. Considering that it can take more than ten separate treatments for a patient to finish the removal process, the cost can add up to thousands of dollars.
- According to the IAPAM, from 2011 to 2012 tattoo removal treatments increased by 32 percent, representing one of the fastest-growing procedures in aesthetic medicine.

What You Should Do About Body Piercing and Tattoos

Deliberate Carefully and Do Research

Take your time in order to make a good decision. Think for a long time and be able to articulate clearly to yourself and others why you want to have bodywork done. Never allow others to pressure you into having a tattoo or piercing, and never have one done when you are under the influence of drugs or alcohol. It is not advisable to have a tattoo done at a festival, at the beach, or in any situation where you are acting on impulse.

Do research on the type of work you want done. The viewpoints in this book can provide some guidance, and many publications will be available at your local library or online. See what medical professionals have to say about the particular procedure that interests you. Ask older people who have tattoos or piercings, especially if they have a lot of them, who they recommend to do the work or which studios they think are the cleanest. Do a lot of studio visits and ask questions. Involve your parents in this discussion. They may ask questions that will save your life. You also will want to do some research on the chemical content of any tattoo inks, many of which are known to be toxic. The Food and Drug Administration does not regulate their manufacturers. Finally, you might take a moment to review your state's laws and regulations of the tattoo and piercing industries, and to see if there are any recent news stories about violations or test cases.

Be Aware of Your Overall Health

As you prepare to have a body piercing or tattoo, also consider whether you have any medical conditions that might rule out certain kinds of bodywork. Does your body or that of anyone in your family form keloid scars? Do you have congenital heart problems? Do you take medications or require medical procedures (such as MRIs) that might interfere with proper healing, or that might interact with chemicals in the inks? Do you have allergies that might be triggered by bodywork? If you have diabetes or another chronic illness that affects autoimmune functioning, it is good to be cognizant of the fact that tattoos and piercings can have an effect on your health. In such cases you will want to consult with your physician before committing to any procedure. Diabetics should be aware that blood-sugar levels and blood pressure will change during the process of having a tattoo, and they should limit the amount of time spent having work done. This means smaller tattoos or tattoos done in shorter sessions. Also, diabetics should avoid having work done on parts of the body with poor circulation—such as the buttocks, ankles, shins, and feet—or anywhere injections are normally delivered.

Check Your Routine

Think through how the bodywork will affect your daily life, and how anything you do on a day-to-day basis might affect the healing process. Consider whether you are involved in work, hobbies, or sports that might require you to remove a piece of jewelry from a piercing before it is healed, thus increasing the opportunity for exposure to infection.

Check Credentials and Know Safety Guidelines

If you decide to have a procedure done, make sure that the person you choose is trained and certified by his professional association. Never allow an untrained amateur to tattoo or pierce your body. Do research on the practitioner and the clinic. Ask for referrals. Ask about his or her policy for the tools used. Visit the clinic ahead of time and take a good look around, paying attention to cleanliness and procedure. Check with the Better Business Bureau or consumer protection agencies in your state to make sure there are no complaints about the business.

A proper professional should verify your age and ask for written consent from your parents if you are a minor and can be legally tattooed or pierced in your state. He or she should wash his or her own hands and clean your skin before and after the procedure. During the procedure he or she should use sterile instruments, taken from sealed packages, wear gloves and other protective coverings, and follow proper guidelines to prevent contamination and the spread of disease. Afterward, he or she should clean all non-disposable equipment with an autoclave, or, for items like drawer handles, with a commercial disinfectant or bleach solution. He or she should provide you with written instructions for care and cleaning of your tattoo or piercing.

Caring for Bodywork

Monitor the site of the procedure closely and follow the cleaning and care directions you are given. If an area that has been tattooed or pierced seems slow to heal, displays swelling or redness, or produces a pus discharge, seek medical help. Infection can spread quickly, and in some parts of the body it can take a long time to clear. Some things you can do to keep your tattoo or piercing free of infection are as follows: Remove the bandage after twenty-four hours, use antibiotic ointment on tattoos or antibiotic wash on piercings, and avoid exposing the areas to sun. Clean tattoos by patting, not rubbing, using a gentle soap and water and avoiding directly spraying water on them. Use a gentle moisturizer on tattoos.

For oral piercings, use nonalcohol mouth rinses such as Biotène or a packaged, sterile saline solution after each meal. Do not use an old toothbrush after having an oral piercing! Have a new soft one ready before you come home. Do not swim or go in hot tubs until any tattooed or pierced areas have healed (at least two weeks for tattoos). Choose clothing that will not stick to the area or catch on jewelry. Do not pick at the area, and do not remove the jewelry until the piercing has healed.

For piercings, use good quality jewelry that is nickel-free. Look for pieces that are surgical steel, titanium, or 14- or 18-carat gold. Make sure you choose pieces of the proper size and of an appropriate function for the body part.

ORGANIZATIONS TO CONTACT

The editors have compiled the following list of organizations concerned with the issues debated in this book. The descriptions are derived from materials provided by the organizations. All have publications or information available for interested readers. The list was compiled on the date of publication of the present volume; the information provided here may change. Be aware that many organizations take several weeks or longer to respond to inquiries, so allow as much time as possible.

Alliance of Professional Tattooists, Inc. (APT)
215 W. 18th Street
Kansas City, MO 64108
(816) 979-1300
website: www.safe-tattoos.com

The APT has as its mission a focus on "preserving the art of tattoo through education, knowledge and awareness." The organization was founded as a nonprofit in 1992 in order to address health and safety issues in the tattoo industry. According to the APT, its efforts were the first of their kind to bring organized health and safety education and standardized infection-control procedures to the industry. The organization was founded in part out of the increasing popularity of tattoos and the resultant greater public scrutiny of tattoo safety and standards.

American Academy of Dermatology (AAD)
1445 New York Ave., NW, Suite 800
Washington, DC 20005
(866) 503-7546 • fax: (847) 240-1859
website: www.aad.org

The AAD was founded in 1938. Today the organization has a membership of more than seventeen thousand, making it the largest dermatology group in the United States. Many international dermatologists and virtually all American dermatologists are represented by the organization. The AAD hosts an annual meeting for members and publishes the *Journal of the American Academy of Dermatology*, both of which contribute to its mission of advancing education, research, and advocacy.

American Academy of Micropigmentation (AAM)
741 N. Kalaheo Ave.
Kailua, HI 96734
(800) 441-2515 • fax: (949) 709-4751
website: www.micropigmentation.org

The AAM is a nonprofit organization dedicated to providing continuing education and national board certification for professionals in the field of permanent makeup and cosmetic tattooing. Founded in 1992, the organization began offering board examinations in 1994 and by 2002 had begun administering the exams in Korean, Japanese, and Spanish translation. The AAM's continuing medical education program offers online modules for its members and provides instructor certification for permanent makeup professionals in the industry. The organization has a subsidiary called the International Micropigmentation Association that provides industry examinations and quality assurance outside the United States.

American Society for Aesthetic Plastic Surgery (ASAPS)
11262 Monarch Street
Garden Grove, CA 92841
(212) 921-0500 • fax: (212) 921-0011
website: www.surgery.org

The ASAPS is a professional organization of board-certified plastic surgeons specializing in cosmetic plastic surgery. The organization was founded in 1967 and now counts a membership of more than 2,600 surgeons from the United States, Canada, and other countries. The mission of the ASAPS focuses primarily on education. Medical education provided by the organization includes sponsorship of scientific meetings and publication of a scientific journal. The ASAPS also supports research and data collection on cosmetic surgery and publishes annual statistics related to its findings. Its public interest and patient advocacy activities include developing relationships with the news media and providing information on cosmetic surgery to the public through its website.

American Society for Dermatologic Surgery (ASDS)
5550 Meadowbrook Drive, Suite 120
Rolling Meadows, IL 60008
(847) 956-0900 • fax: (847) 956-0999
website: www.asds.net

The ASDS is a member organization of more than 5,800 specialists in dermatologic surgery and intervention. The organization provides a variety of services to its members that aim to promote their expertise and leadership in the field of cosmetic and medically necessary skin treatment and surgery. Such services include annual meetings that provide continuing education and training, networking forums, mentorship programs, and a specialty journal. The ASDS also advocates on behalf of its members' interests to set related health care policy, and prepares public awareness activities.

Association of Professional Piercers (APP)
PO Box 1287
Lawrence, KS 66044
(888) 888-1277 • fax: (267) 482-5650
website: www.safepiercing.org

The APP was formed in 1994 in response to concerns about legislation proposals in California. The political action group that formed out of this event brought together a variety of piercing studios and soon broadened its scope to address the needs of the piercing profession in the United States and internationally. The organizational structure includes a voluntary elected board of directors and its membership includes piercing professionals from around the world. The focus of the APP is to provide current and accurate information and education on body piercing both for industry specialists and for interested parties such as legislators, health care professionals, and the general public.

Centers for Disease Control and Prevention (CDC)
1600 Clifton Road
Atlanta, GA 30333
(404) 639-3311
website: www.cdc.gov

The CDC is the main health agency of the US government. The mission of the CDC is to promote health and quality of life by preventing and controlling disease, injury, and disability. The CDC provides up-to-date information to the public on health and diseases. The agency publishes several journals, including *Emerging Infectious Diseases* and *Morbidity and Mortality Weekly Report*.

Council of Better Business Bureaus (CBBB)
3033 Wilson Blvd., Suite 600
Arlington, VA 22201
(703) 276-0100
website: www.bbb.org/council

The CBBB is the national council that oversees regional organizations, known as Better Business Bureaus, which are tasked with creating an ethical marketplace for American consumers. BBB is dedicated to setting marketplace standards; identifying, investigating, and publicizing businesses that perpetrate consumer scams and profit from unethical behavior in the marketplace; encouraging and supporting best practices; offering objective and accurate information to the public on businesses and the marketplace; and denouncing businesses that violate BBB standards. If an organization has received BBB accreditation, it means that it has been vetted and found to meet BBB's standard of performance and service. The BBB website offers information for consumers on accredited businesses and charities, key articles and tips for consumers, lists of the top consumer scams of the year, a blog, and access to the BBB's e-newsletters, including *Scam Alert*, *Smart Investing*, and *Wise Giving*.

Homeboy Industries
130 W. Bruno Street
Los Angeles, CA 90012
(323) 526-1254 • fax: (323) 526-1257
website: www.homeboyindustries.org

Homeboy Industries provides a variety of services to at-risk men and women with gang-related histories. The organization was founded in Los Angeles in 1988 to address the city's escalating gang violence and now provides a number of services alongside its social enterprise job training programs. Its tattoo removal services are critical for former gang members seeking reentry into the workforce or schools, and are provided free of charge by a team of volunteer doctors. This is often the first service that is requested by new clients to the organization, and many times leads to a greater involvement in Homeboy Industries' other gang rehabilitation programs.

National Tattoo Association, Inc. (NTA)
485 Business Park Lane
Allentown, PA 18109
(610) 433-7261
website: www.nationaltattooassociation.com

The NTA was founded in 1976, became a nonprofit organization in 1978, and held its first national convention in 1979 in Denver, Colorado. The organization aims to bring greater awareness to tattoos as an art form. Its membership includes tattoo artists from around the world, and contests are held at the annual conventions to recognize the excellence of the tattoo artist participants. Since its founding, the NTA's scope has come to include a complementary focus on quality, safety standards, and professionalism in the tattoo community.

Society of Permanent Cosmetic Professionals (SPCP)
69 N. Broadway Street
Des Plaines, IL 60016
(847) 635-1330 • fax: (847) 635-1326
website: www.spcp.org

The SPCP promotes "permanent makeup safety, excellence, and professional standards by providing education, certification, and industry guidelines." The organization's membership is open to anyone who agrees to abide by its code of conduct, and includes professionals and others who are involved in the industry of permanent cosmetics, also known as cosmetic tattooing. The SPCP also assures standards of practice in cosmetic tattooing by administering a competency examination to become recognized as a Certified Permanent Cosmetic Professional.

US Food and Drug Administration (FDA)
10903 New Hampshire Ave.
Silver Spring, MD 20993
(888) 463-6332
website: www.fda.gov

The FDA is one of the nation's oldest consumer protection agencies. Its mission is to promote and protect the public health by helping safe and effective products reach the market in a timely way; by monitoring products for continued safety after they are in use; and by helping the public get the accurate, science-based information needed to improve health. Aside from food and tobacco, the FDA is also responsible for oversight of human and veterinary drugs, medical devices, and cosmetics, which include the pigments and dies in permanent and temporary tattoos.

BIBLIOGRAPHY

Books

Elayne Angel, *The Piercing Bible: Guide to Aftercare and Trouble-shooting.* Berkeley, CA: Crossing Press e-book, 2013.

Robert Arp, *Tattoos–Philosophy for Everyone: I Ink, Therefore I Am.* Hoboken, NJ: Wiley-Blackwell, 2012.

Gregory Boyle, *Tattoos on the Heart: The Power of Boundless Compassion.* New York: Free Press, 2010.

Leanne Currie-McGhee, *Tattoos, Body Piercings, and Health.* San Diego: Reference Point, 2013.

Christa De Cuyper and Maria-Luisa Pérez-Cotapos, eds., *Dermatologic Complications with Body Art: Tattoos, Piercings and Permanent Make-Up.* Heidelberg, Germany: Springer, 2010.

Margo Demello, *Body Studies: An Introduction.* Oxford and New York: Routledge, 2014.

Sherri Elliott, *Ties to Tattoos: Turning Generational Differences into a Competitive Advantage.* Dallas: Brown Books, 2009.

Armando Favazza, *Bodies Under Siege: Self-Mutilation, Nonsuicidal Self-Injury, and Body Modification in Culture and Psychiatry,* 3rd ed. Baltimore: Johns Hopkins University Press, 2011.

Karen Hudson, *Living Canvas: Your Total Guide to Tattoos, Piercings, and Body Modification.* Berkeley, CA: Seal Press, 2009.

Alessandra Lemma, *Under the Skin: A Psychoanalytic Study of Body Modification.* London and New York: Routledge/Taylor and Francis, 2010.

Margot Mifflin, *Bodies of Subversion: A Secret History of Women and Tattoo,* 3rd revised ed. New York: PowerHouse, 2013.

Xichao Mo, *My Victory Against Vitiligo: A Successful Story and a Practical Guide to Treatment.* Boynton Beach, FL: Paclinx, 2014.

Aliesh Pierce, *Milady's Aesthetician Series: Treating Diverse Pigmentation*. Clifton Park, NY: Milady/Cengage, 2013.

Lisiunia A. Romanienko, *Body Piercing and Identity Construction: A Comparative Perspective*. New York: Palgrave Macmillan, 2011.

Laura Vegas, *Straight Talk About Body Piercing*. Amazon e-book, 2010.

Periodicals and Internet Sources

Josh Adams, "Marked Difference: Tattooing and Its Association with Deviance in the United States," *Deviant Behavior*, vol. 30, no. 3, 2009, pp. 266–92.

"America's Booming Tattoo Economy: By the Numbers," *The Week*, September 20, 2012. www.theweek.com.

"Body Modification and Body Image," The Body Project, Bradley University, 2014. www.bradley.edu.

Mark Burgess and Louise Clark, "Do the 'Savage Origins' of Tattoos Cast a Prejudicial Shadow on Contemporary Tattooed Individuals?," *Journal of Applied Social Psychology*, vol. 40, no. 3, March 2010, pp. 746–64.

Richard Dukes and Judith Stein, "Ink and Holes: Correlates and Predictive Associations of Body Modification Among Adolescents," *Youth and Society*, vol. 43, no. 4, 2011, pp. 1,547–69.

Adam Clark Estes, "The Freaky, Bioelectric Future of Tattoos," *Gizmodo*, January 6, 2014. www.gizmodo.com.

Amanda Haddaway, "Hiring Discrimination Against Tattoos and Piercings," October 14, 2013. www.careerealism.com.

Rachel Hennessey, "Tattoos No Longer a Kiss of Death in the Workplace," *Forbes*, February 27, 2013. www.forbes.com.

Lauren Hise, "When Body Piercings Can Pose Major Health Risks," Medill Reports–Chicago, Northwestern University, February 16, 2012. http://news.medill.northwestern.edu.

Tony Isaacs, "Bad News for Tattoos—Many Tattoo Inks Contain Dangerous Heavy Metals, Phthalates and Hydrocarbons," *Natural News*, January 21, 2014. www.naturalnews.com.

Karin Lehner et al., "Black Tattoo Inks Are a Source of Problematic Substances Such as Dibutyl Phthalate," *Contact Dermatitis*, vol. 65, no. 4, October 2011.

Eric Madfis and Tammi Arford, "The Dilemmas of Embodied Symbolic Representation: Regret in Contemporary American Tattoo Narratives," *Social Science Journal*, vol. 50, no. 4, October 2013, pp. 547–56.

Joyce M. Miller and Joyce Fitzpatrick, "Patient Education: Piercing: Does Health Education Make a Difference?," *Nurse Practitioner: The American Journal of Primary Healthcare*, vol. 35, no. 6, June 2010, pp. 48–52. www.nursingcenter.com.

Grie Verd, "Spiritual Punk—a Tattooed Woman Goes Home to God," April 17, 2013. http://quiescentbeing.wordpress.com.

Sharon Worcester, "Nickel, Cobalt Sensitivity Increases with Number of Body Piercings," *Skin and Allergy News*, April 15, 2013. www.skinandallergynews.com.

INDEX

A
Adults
  ear, face, body piercings data, *51*
  long-term body art data, 67–68
  sexual activity-tattoo connection, 69
  tattoo-related regrets, 61
  US tattoo data, 6, 9, *19*, *25*, 27, 38–39
  See also Parents
Age for getting tattoos, 55–58
American Academy of Dermatology, 63
American Medical Association (AMA), 6
American Society for Dermatologic Surgery (ASDS), 61
Angel, Elayne, 44–45
Association of Professional Piercers (APP), 44–45
Astrological sign tattoo, 57
Avitzur, Orly, 38–42

B
Back/buttocks tattoo, 11
Bieber, Justin, 38
Black henna
  bad reactions, 36–37
  temporary tattoo risk factors, *34*, 35

Blood-borne pathogens, 11
Bodies of Subversion: A Secret History of Women and Tattoo (Mifflin), 9
Body piercings
  adult piercing data, *51*
  avoidance recommendations, 47–48, 50–53
  complications, *39*
  consequences of forcing, 46–47
  infection risks, 11, 40, 46
  job discrimination, 71–74
  judgments against pierced people, 5
  nose piercing, 6–7, 20, 45–46
  self-care role, 18–21, 24–26
  standard safety precautions, 44–45
  therapeutic value, 20–21
  tongue piercing, 45–46
  See also Ear piercing

C
California
  legal age for tattoos, 55, 57
  tattoo shop regulations, 11
  tattoo shops, 9–11
Cardona-Tapia, Silvia, 55–58
Cartilage (aka Barbie), 53–54
Centers for Disease Control and Prevention (CDC), 28

92

Stretching. *See* Ear stretching

Survival struggles, tattoo representations, 13–17

Swartz, Susan, 8–12

Symbol tattoos, 19

T

Tattoo artists (tattooists)
  career choice popularity, 66–67
  licensing requirements, 40
  OSHA courses, certifications, 11
  safe inking procedures, 40–43, *41*
  throw-away kits, 42

Tattoo removal
  costs/time commitment, 6, 11, 63–64
  dermabrasion method, 61–62
  do-it-yourself ointments, 62–63
  laser technology, 61, *62*
  limitations, 63
  reasons, *60*
  US FDA recommendations, 59–64

Tattooed workers by industry, *72*

Tattoos
  choice of images vs. words, *16*
  empowerment value, *23*
  growing mainstream popularity, 8–12, *19*
  identity-assertion value, 18–26

identity-seeking value, 13–17

ink-related infections, 27–32

pre-tattoo preparation, 38–43

risks, *29*

self-care role, 18–21

social branding value, 65–70

state laws for minors, 55, 56, 57, 58

teen tattoo rights, 55–58

therapeutic value, 17, 20–21

Temporary tattoos
  black henna, bad reactions, 36–37
  black henna, dangers, 35
  risk factors, 33–35
  types, *36t*

Therapeutic value
  body piercings, 20–21
  tattoos, 17, 20–21

Tongue piercing, 45–46

Torso piercing, 47

Tramp stamp, 53, 65

Triangle Tattoo Art and Museum, 9–10

U

US Department of Justice, 31

US Food and Drug Administration (FDA), 28, *30*
  laser device tattoo removal approval, 61
  risk-reduction collaborations, 28, 31
  tattoo removal recommendations, 59–64

temporary tattoo risk factors,
33–37
Uvula piercing, 47

V
Verret, D.J., 47

W
Wilder, Kate, 8, 11

Women
    increased favoring of tattoos,
        9
    men tattoo comparison, 6, 39
    stud piercing, 53
    tattoo removal frequency, 69

PICTURE CREDITS